MANAGER AS COACH

The New Way to Get Results

MANAGER AS COACH

The New Way to Get Results

Jenny Rogers

with

**Andrew Gilbert and
Karen Whittleworth**

 **Professional**

McGraw-Hill Education
McGraw-Hill House
Shoppenhangers Road
Maidenhead
Berkshire
England
SL6 2QL

and Two Penn Plaza, New York, NY 10121-2289, USA

First published 2012

A catalogue record of this book is available from the British Library

ISBN-13: 978-0-077-14018-2 (pb)
ISBN-10: 0-077-14018-4 (pb)
eISBN: 978-0-077-14019-9

Library of Congress Cataloging-in-Publication Data
CIP data applied for

Typesetting and e-book compilations by RefineCatch Limited, Bungay, Suffolk
Printed and bound by CPI Group (UK) Ltd, Croydon, CR0 4YY

Fictitious names of companies, products, people, characters and/or data that may be used herein (in case studies or in examples) are not intended to represent any real individual, company, product or event.

The McGraw·Hill Companies

Jenny Rogers is one of the leading executive coaches in the UK with more than 20 years of experience. Her clients are typically chief executives and directors of large organizations. She writes extensively about coaching and leadership and has trained many hundreds of managers in coaching skills in the UK and internationally.

Karen Whittleworth is an acclaimed trainer, coach and coach supervisor, and the founding director of Worth Consulting Ltd.

Andrew Gilbert is an internationally known speaker, trainer and executive coach. He is the co-director of Worth Consulting Ltd.

From JR:
For my sons, Luke and Owen

From AG and KW:
To our sons, Henry and Oliver. We hope this book helps you as leaders in your new business ventures.

CONTENTS

xi

INTRODUCTION: IT'S TOUGH BEING A BOSS

It's a tough job being a manager. At the heart of why this is are two demands that might appear totally at odds. They go like this:

> *Set high standards, be in control.* We're not living in those easy-going, soft times any more. You're accountable for the performance of your staff. Challenge hard if you can see that they're under-performing.

And at the same time . . .

> *Be nice, give away your power.* You don't get good performance out of people by being tough, and in any case staff today won't tolerate being told what to do. It's your job to encourage them.

How are these apparent opposites to be reconciled?

If you come across as too directive and demanding, you may get a reputation for harshness and may even find that formal grievances are being laid against you. If you are too nice, you will be known as a gullible sucker, easily out-manoeuvred, with the additional tweak that if your staff make mistakes you will be held responsible. No wonder, then, that so many of the managers we work with overdo one style and at the same time neglect the other or else flip confusingly between the two. It is rare to find someone who is comfortable balancing the two. High rank and experience do not seem to make a great deal of difference. Many of our most senior executive coaching clients, some of them well known enough to be the focus of newspaper profiles and stories, can struggle with these issues as fiercely as any of their most junior counterparts.

In this book, we describe how coaching can be a major part of the solution. We start by challenging many of the traditional assumptions about what works in management – for instance, that appraisal systems can manage performance, something that research has amply demonstrated to be untrue. We offer you a simple definition of what coaching is, showing how it can motivate people as well as being a way of managing their performance. The book will give you step-by-step guidance on coaching skills and many examples of how it can be used in everyday managerial situations.

As coaching has become more popular, so its currency has been devalued. We train many managers who sincerely believe they are already coaching their staff. The more senior they are, the more likely they are to believe they have nothing to learn in this respect and the less likely their subordinates are to challenge them. They attend a training course reluctantly or with a benign wish to share their brilliance as coaches with other course members:

> I felt extreme irritation at having to give up time to do this coaching course but decided I should go in order to set a good example and because my Learning & Development manager more or less told me that it would undermine the whole programme if I refused. I thought I already had all the coaching skills I needed and I planned to develop a sudden illness at the end of day 1. By the end of day 1 I had discovered that I had never truly coached my staff, that it was all a great deal trickier and more subtle than I thought, and that the power of real coaching was far, far greater than I had ever imagined.

This person, the chief executive in a large company, was first surprised, then humbled, and finally totally captivated by the potential of what he had discovered, went on to complete a coaching qualification and to set a powerful example to the rest of his executive team.

This participant's experience is a reminder of how important it is for coaching to percolate the whole organization and not just to be private knowledge shared between those who are in on the secret. In Chapter 9, we describe how to create a coaching culture, where coaching is the thread that runs through every interaction in the organization, whether with staff, suppliers or customers. This is a major undertaking and we know of no organizations that have yet achieved this starry status, but we do know of many that are on their way and that can already point to its multiple benefits for the bottom line.

This bottom line perspective is important. Coaching is not a fluffy nice-to-have. The point about coaching is that it creates engagement and engagement creates great bottom line results, never more vital than now, when economic misery threatens the survival of so many previously healthy organizations.

Why our OSCAR model works

In training thousands of managers over the years, we realized that they needed a coaching model that would get to the heart of any manager's dilemma: how to get results that will stick; how to improve performance without either bullying or just doing nothing and hoping for the best. We noticed that professional coaches could use any coaching model with ease. However, managers looking to use a coaching style but not looking to become professional coaches had a little more trouble. In particular, managers have to assess risk and manage performance in a way that professional coaches do not. That is why we developed a simple way of memorizing a framework for any coaching conversation. We call this OSCAR, which stands for Outcome, Situation, Choices and Consequences, Action, and Review.

The O (Outcome) and S (Situation) of OSCAR are similar to the well known GROW model (Goal, Reality, Options, Way forward). But introducing the C (Choices and Consequences) element of OSCAR makes it more suited to management. By exploring the upsides and downsides, risk can be explored more thoroughly. Risk can be defined as anything that could prevent you achieving your desired outcome. Every decision is a choice. Wisdom can be defined as the ability to anticipate the consequences of your choices in advance of making them. OSCAR facilitates wise choices by treating upsides and downsides (reward and risk) equally.

The OSCAR model recognizes that for a manager, the buck stops with them. The manager is ultimately responsible for the performance of their staff. The R (Review) part of OSCAR is a much firmer process for a manager than the Way forward part of GROW. Agreeing when and how actions will be reviewed removes the option of not taking action. Staff members are normally perfectly genuine when they agree to perform some action. But people work in environments with sharply competing priorities, and how they prioritize largely comes down to what they believe will be noticed and what they believe will be ignored. Why do some managers find that their staff pay lip service to actions while other managers don't? The critical factor is the manager's skill in reviewing. A boss who takes a coaching approach and also agrees a review point – and sticks to it – finds that the actions get taken.

We have written this book from a shared passion about the importance of coaching as a new way of behaving as a manager, one that gets results and aligns people to what the organization needs. Everything we have written is based on evidence, on our experience as managers ourselves, and on coaching and training many thousands of managers in coaching skills. Our intention is, to paraphrase Albert

Einstein, to make it as simple as possible but not too simple. We give many dozens of real-life examples, some recounted or written by named clients, others with details and names disguised.

By using OSCAR consistently, you become the manager whose deadlines cannot be ignored. You become the boss whose loyal team magically seem to get all their work done. You know what is happening on the ground because, thanks to the relationships you create with your team through coaching, they are fearless in telling you. You can take quick decisive action when necessary. You can inspire through shared goals.

Find out how to do this by reading the rest of this book.

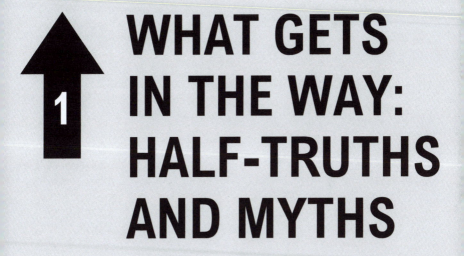

WHAT GETS IN THE WAY: HALF-TRUTHS AND MYTHS

1

In this chapter, we look at some of the most common half-truths and myths about what it takes to be a boss. We explore how deep-rooted such beliefs are – for instance, that bonuses will improve performance – and how they persist despite evidence that they are a poor basis for managing people effectively. What stands in the way of finding sensible solutions to the problems of how to get good work out of people without either bullying or being too soft on them? Our own belief is that at least some of the real culprits are some of the familiar assumptions about management, many of which are rarely challenged.

Management as a profession is only just over 100 years old. Before the early years of the twentieth century, industrial organizations were still relatively small, typically based in just one location. Expansion, prosperity, and economic growth meant that old ways of organizing labour were not necessarily going to be right.

Two influences had a major impact.

Military culture

In the nineteenth and early twentieth centuries, armies were among the few examples of large organizations and were often a raggle-taggle of poorly educated conscripts or else mercenaries whose loyalty could not be assumed. An army is in a state of emergency: its members face defeat and death, so it is essential for clear orders to be given and to have a crisp, reliable way of controlling potential chaos. The default way of doing this was brute force. So, for instance, in the British Army of the First World War, soldiers – including those suffering what we would now call post-traumatic stress disorder – were shot for 'cowardice' by their own side. The poor quality of leadership, so aptly summed up in the scornful phrase 'lions led by donkeys' and the tragic stupidity of this war, was not enough on its own to professionalize the British Army. Daft rules traditionally prevailed, as did meaningless activities like 'square bashing', marching around to fill in the time with a sergeant major bawling at you for minor infringements of the 'correct' posture or uniform and with humiliating punishments for breaching the rules.

Military service must have had a pervasive influence given the hundreds of thousands of men and women who were exposed to it in the middle years of the twentieth century, not just through war but through National Service. For instance, it was, and still is, part of the tradition of most boys' public schools to have a Cadet Corps, a pretend-army of lads whose marching and unloaded guns are assumed to be character shaping. We should also consider the Scouting movement for young people, a continuing phenomenal success with wholly benign aims. Its founder, Robert Baden Powell, was a Lieutenant-General in the British Army. Softened down and heavily informalized though Scouting is now, the young members still wear what are in effect military uniforms: khaki, navy or airforce blue with badges standing in for medals. Badges today have a nice line in offhand humour ('I'm a cool camper'; 'Toastin' Marshmallows') but the metaphors are military: clubs are called troops and have patrols led by patrol leaders.

If you feel a sense of superiority about your distance from this, have you ever thought about why you wear that dark suit with the squared shoulders, sharply angled collar, and neatly shaped silhouette to an important meeting, job interview or presentation? The underlying visual metaphor is undoubtedly the military uniform of an officer. If you are a woman, wear something pastel or flowery to such events at peril of seeming girlish; if you are a man, and turn up over-casually dressed in chinos and a polo shirt you will risk being dismissed similarly as a lightweight.

Modern armies are very different places, but the influence of the old ideas lingers on somewhere in our collective subconscious and has affected many of the approaches to management that persist today: telling rather than negotiating, minutely crafted differences in hierarchy, engaging in pointless busyness, imposing uniforms on staff who don't really need them, and creating petty rules in the name of 'discipline'. You should note, too, the frequency with which military metaphors appear in corporate communications: staff are 'troops', there will be 'war' on competitors, the strategy will have 'weapons' with which to 'fight', some of which may be 'the nuclear option'.

Frederick Taylor and scientific management

For much of the rest, we lay at least some of the responsibility on Frederick Taylor (1856–1915), whose experiments at the US company Bethlehem Steel in the late nineteenth century have been the foundation of so many of today's assumptions about how to be a manager, even though for a man who has had so much impact on our lives, few people today have heard of him. Taylor watched men shovelling coal at the steelworks and noticed how much more efficient some were than others. By standing over them with a stopwatch and keen sense of observation, he realized there was an optimum time and method. His recommendations to the steelworks bosses reduced headcount by 72 per cent, cut costs, and increased profits. It seemed so obvious: you applied rational analysis and made change happen.

Taylor believed in the 'scientific' division of labour. Change had to be imposed – workers were incapable of understanding or being trusted with their tasks. In 'scientific management', the label he gave his ideas, the workforce was to be treated like a machine. There would be 'one right way', everything depending on unambiguous centralized control, and the one right way was devised and *enforced* (a favourite word) by the new profession of *manager*, people who did not do any shovelling themselves, but simply organized others and made sure they did what they were told. Time-and-motion, the method he developed, was the predecessor of the far more humane Business Process Re-engineering (but note the metaphor, an assumption that organizations are machines) of the late twentieth century and, as it turns out, equally ineffective.

The theory was attractive: what employer would not like to have a dramatic increase in output at the same time as reducing costs? The trouble was that mostly, whenever time-and-motion was introduced, strikes and protests followed, as indeed they have ever since.

Taylor's influence has been pervasive. When his methods have not worked, the assumption has usually been that they need to be applied with more force – thus doing more of what does not work. If you doubt Taylor's influence, consider this: Is your organization one that sets objectives and then expects them to cascade downwards? Does your boss set yours? Do you have – and give – performance appraisals? Do you struggle to delegate effectively? Do you work long hours and most weekends? Do you have efficiency targets? Do you get an individual performance bonus? The more of these questions you answer 'yes', the more likely it is that you are a direct inheritor of Frederick Taylor's legacy.

Along with the legacies from Taylor and the military, there are some deeply ingrained beliefs and assumptions about management, many of which, when subjected to research and close examination, turn out to be only half true or just plain wrong. The following are some of the most common.

Assumption: Human beings are rational, so you can manage through rationality

The discoveries of neuroscience are revolutionizing our understanding of essential human functioning and over-turning much that was previously thought to be a given. The human brain is unique in that we have a bigger layer of prefrontal cortex cells than any other land animal. This layer enables us to plan, to use language, to think strategically, to weigh up one option against another – in other words to be 'rational'. However, we flatter ourselves if we believe that the prefrontal cortex is dominant, because it is not. The function of the human brain is to rationalize, not to be rational. This is because the dominant part of our brain is the limbic system, the seat of emotion and memory. Although its work-ings are outside conscious awareness, it governs all our decision-making. If you doubt this, consider for a moment how you made any of the important decisions in your life – for instance, whether to marry, invest in a course of educa-tion, have a child, leave or take up a job, move house, make any kind of major purchase. You will have decided on the basis of feelings, though you probably justified the decisions with a logical argument later. So in managerial terms, it is entirely hopeless to assume that giving people the logical case – for instance, about why the organization needs to shed jobs – will be convincing. Our first and most powerful responses are always emotional. Successful managers are people who know and can work with this. They are able to manage their own and other people's emotions with aplomb.

Assumption: Personal life belongs at home

There are innumerable variants of this belief, including that it is not 'appropriate' for managers to discuss the home lives of their staff or to disclose their own. On many occasions our clients have assured us that they 'leave feelings at home'. If only: the feelings are there all right, but usually suppressed, with enormous difficulty, under a mask of one kind or another.

Until the early twentieth century, work and home were indivisible. Home was also the workplace and work was woven into the life of the local community. But now there seems to be a strange belief that the fundamental laws of human interaction somehow do not – or should not – apply at work. In most organizations, you are supposed to focus entirely on its needs and forget your obligations to family and friends. There can be severe penalties for making private phone calls and emails or for *cyberslacking* (using the Internet). Along with this assumption, that work and home are totally different and played to different rules, is the expectation of very long hours. This is how one young lawyer described the common practices in his large firm of City solicitors:

> If you're under thirty and just qualified you get all the grunt work. Sixteen-hour days are the norm for me. I am too tired to go home at least one night a week and I keep a sleeping bag at the office now. I sleep on the floor under my desk.

In fact it makes far more sense to embrace home with work. It's the same person who comes to work as the one who goes home later. What is happening in our private lives has a major impact on our work lives and vice versa, so if your child is seriously ill, it is most unlikely that you will be able to remain unworried at work or that your concentration will not be affected. If you have a row with a colleague, the chances are you will take the feelings of misery home with you. Contrary to common assumptions, it makes commercial sense to understand that part of your role as a manager is to understand as much as staff feel able to trust you with as far as their home lives go and for you to be able to do the same with them.

If you have to pretend to be someone different at work, the cost of such inauthenticity is high:

> I worked in telesales after leaving university because I was desperate for a job. Everything we did was recorded, there was constant monitoring of how long calls were taking and what our success rate was, and how 'aggressively' we had pursued our targets. I went home despising myself. I put on masses of weight because I was comfort eating, I felt alienated from everything that was important to me, and knew I couldn't take it for more than a few months. I fantasized about leaving the whole time and my work got worse and worse.

By contrast, many of the world's most profitable companies, such as 3M, encourage authenticity, and indeed hire for it. Part of the extraordinary success of companies like Southwest Airlines is the permeability of the boundaries between work and home, with families routinely invited to social events and with work–home balance formally acknowledged as a corporate value. Innovative companies such as Google are renowned for the way they design office environments that invite play – the opposite of the typically formal grey, cellular office environments of the late twentieth century. Young people entering work now have grown up with technology. They are used to doing work-like activities at home and expect the same kind of flexibility from work. At many of the most innovative organizations such as Pixar, creators of the wildly successful *Toy Story* franchise and makers of awesomely creative, polished, and profitable work, there are no corporate uniforms either formal or informal – what people wear at home, they wear to work. A piece introducing an article about the company in the *New Yorker* magazine[1] describes part of what their writer saw. Here some of their most seriously talented – and possibly craziest – people have in fact created home at work, with every encouragement from their employers.

> The funkiest parish is where the animators, a hundred and twenty in number, dwell, and where their fancies are encouraged to sprout. Each den is decorated in accordance with the whim, or the exotic id, of its occupant; thus, one has a Tiki theme, another is lined with Japanese movie posters, and several are built inside garden sheds. (If you want to see the opposite of this, a sum of all Pixar's fears, watch the office scenes in 'The Incredibles,' directed by Brad Bird, where the vast Bob Parr, alias Mr. Incredible, crouches wretchedly in the mouse-gray box of his workspace.

Of course there are limits to what it is appropriate or realistic for a manager to discuss with staff (we discuss some of them on p. 268), but the fact remains that it makes good sense to know at least a little about what is going on for people outside work.

Assumption: Leaders can be in control

Healthy organizations need control systems, otherwise there would be chaos, but this is not the same as any one person or group of people being in control. Control systems work best when they are distributed and based on widely shared values. Control is largely a mirage, but it may in so many organizations be a mirage shared by staff and seniors alike. The writer Peter Senge provides a vivid description of why in practice it is impossible to control an organization:

> Imagine you have two roller skates attached to each other by a spring. You use the first roller skate to control the movement of the second. It's a bit tricky but doable. Now add a third roller skate, attached with another spring . . . Now try to control the third roller skate by moving only the first . . . Keep adding roller skates, each attached by springs with different spring constants. It doesn't take long to give up any hope of controlling the roller skate at the far end of the line. Organizations are infinitely more complex than this simple line of roller skates. You can begin to see why one person dictating orders from 'one end of the line' cannot possibly control what happens in a complex organization.
>
> (Senge 1990: 290)

Senge comments that it is easy to confuse giving orders with being in control, and to confuse the lavish salaries and luxurious benefits of those at the top – and the apparent deference they receive – with the ability to influence events. As coaches and consultants, we have frequently worked with chief executives who have discovered that their power was nothing like as extensive as they imagined. For instance, we recall one organization where the chief executive was overheard asking peevishly why there were still no squeezy tomato-shaped ketchup dispensers in the canteens of his offices when he had several times commanded this to happen because he liked them himself. The answer was that he had also issued orders forbidding the purchase of any items of 'frippery' unless they were signed off by three managers in succession. The permission for the squeezy tomatoes had got lost somewhere in an intricate maze of inboxes deep inside the organization.

Myths about leadership are pervasive in the management literature, whether the 'secrets' of bosses like Jack Welch of General Electric or self-help books like Stephen Covey's *Seven Habits of Highly Effective People* (1989). The belief that leaders make a difference is underlined by the enormous amounts of compensation that bosses of FTSE 500 companies receive – collectively many millions of pounds and often many hundreds of times the average wage of their employees. That leaders can and do make a difference, positive or negative, is plain. Yet the evidence shows that the link between leadership and performance is often modest, perhaps as little as 10 per cent of the difference between a failing and a successful organization because performance is so largely influenced by factors over which leaders have no control, such as the weather, the macroeconomic and political climate, oil prices, wars, currency speculation, and many others.

Power can delude people into believing their own myths and into losing sight of how bizarre their behaviour has become. In one organization, the CEO was often seen barefoot and in one-to-one meetings would commonly floss his teeth or file his nails while idly flicking his TV between channels and dosing himself from a silver flask with unnamed contents. This behaviour was widely discussed in the organization but never challenged.

The delusory sense of entitlement that so often corrupts those in power lies behind the delicious story, sadly totally mythical, which goes something like this:

Captain of large ship to apparent obstacle ship in dense fog (*said in self-important tone*)	Divert your course 10 degrees north immediately to avert collision.

Obstacle (*calmly*)	You should divert your course 10 degrees south to avert collision.
Captain (*angry and irritated*)	You are addressing the captain of the *HMS Blank*, second biggest ship in the Royal Navy, accompanied by two destroyers, two cruisers, and innumerable support vessels. I demand that you divert course immediately 10 degrees north, that's one zero north, otherwise you will be responsible for the consequences.
Obstacle	This is a lighthouse. Suggest you divert YOUR course immediately.

At heart, you can't control others, you can only be certain of controlling yourself. So if controlling others is essentially impossible, the true task of a boss is to create loyalty – and loyalty is given because people like, respect, and admire you. It is given willingly and on the basis of how people experience you as one human being to another. This is why the most successful bosses are people who are confident and also humble; informal, friendly, and accessible yet also have personal dignity and relaxed, natural authority, do not conceal their human flaws and yet have high emotional intelligence along with personal mastery of whatever their area of expertise is.

Assumption: Force works

Force, whether physical or psychological, is at the extreme end of trying to control. In the short term, yes, it is possible to control people, especially if you use intimidation. But longer term it is not. Force can work and of course it does in wars and other conflicts. However, the effort and cost of using force is enormous. If you use your power, mostly you will lose it by seeming unreasonable and overbearing. It only reduces resistance temporarily. In effect, you are just postponing the moment when people fight back. Also, never underestimate the draining impact on the enforcers. Evidence from some of the most extreme of these situations – for instance, the camps of the Holocaust, slavery in the USA, apartheid in South Africa, Stalinist Russia – suggests that it is psychologically and physically exhausting to be a captor. You have to be constantly alert for signs of rebellion and sabotage, the need for human connection is denied (sometimes by the fantasy that the people you are abusing are not really human at all), and you may feel self-disgust about the morality of what the situation requires you to do either at the time or later.

Assumption: Everything should be measured

Measurement was at the heart of Frederick Taylor's approach to management and without measurement of some sort, organizations would be struggling, but the most important factors influencing the success or failure of an organization are intangibles that cannot be measured or put into a spreadsheet. These include:

● *Innovation and creativity*. Essential for continued success, but how would you measure how much or little of it there was in an organization?

- *The future direction of a market.* The most studied systems in the world are the stock market and the weather, but attempts to predict what will happen here in the longer term are invariably wrong, so how much more difficult is it to predict whether any individual product will fail or succeed or whether a market will expand or contract?

- *Motivation.* What gets people up in the mornings? How do you distinguish a motivated from an unmotivated employee? What is it exactly that will create the motivation which means that people will make that desirable extra effort without being asked?

- *Leadership.* What is the magical element that distinguishes a good leader from a mediocre one and from a poor one? Even the very best 'competency analyses' and 360 feedback forms (multiple ratings by colleagues via a questionnaire) cannot actually nail down those elusive qualities

- *The benefits of education and training.* We have to assume that these processes are beneficial, but precise measurement has escaped everyone who has tried, especially their longer-term impact, when so many other variables come into play, though this should not stop us from making educated guesses (see p. 245 for ideas about how to measure the value of coaching).

Assumption: Objectives set at the top can cascade through the organization

In the 1960s and 1970s, there was a school of thought called Management By Objectives (MBO). The idea was that the most senior team introduced objectives for the entire organization: clear targets with timescales and the means of getting there. Objectives would then be cascaded down the various layers of the organization ensuring that every single person had their own objectives and was aligned to overall corporate aims. MBO was a sensible-sounding idea, but the practice has proved a lot more difficult than the theory. It depends for success on assuming that the people at the top know best and can control the people at the bottom, but as was shown above, this is a highly unreliable idea. Perhaps more seriously, objective setting involves guesswork and the assumption that the organization's environment (its competitors, regulators, technology) will all remain the same throughout whatever period of time the objectives are supposed to cover – often a whole year. Given the rapidity of change, this is unlikely and in practice objectives can become immediately outdated by forces entirely outside the control of any individual.

Targets can distort quality. One of the most famous sayings associated with MBO is 'what gets measured is what gets done'. The trouble is that what gets done may not always be the most important thing in the longer term. The quick fix often addresses the symptom and can leave the underlying problem untouched, hence the wisdom of the saying that *today's problems are yesterday's solutions.*

Assumption: Performance appraisals are an essential tool of management

The scene is a conference attended by a large group of managers from a variety of organizations. The presenter asks the question, 'Please raise your hand if a performance appraisal has ever had a beneficial effect on your performance'. Five people out of an audience of 250 put a hand up, to the accompaniment of much foot-shuffling and a ripple of uneasy laughter. Whenever this experiment is repeated, it gets the same result.

The challenge of how to get good performance out of people is invariably about feelings, not logic. But feelings are messy, invisible a lot of the time, and certainly not measureable. When faced with a feelings problem in our fellow humans, our instinct is to try to manage it with a system and then to try to measure its success. This explains what is otherwise inexplicable: why continue to place faith in appraisal systems when it is so obvious that they do not work, never have, and never could? And when it is clear that they are not working – steadily increasing non-compliance by managers being the most frequent problem – why try to solve the problem by inventing a new system that allegedly will solve all the problems of the old one? In many organizations, it would not be uncommon to see at least six such new appraisal systems introduced over a twenty-year period, none any more successful than its predecessors.

The problems with appraisal systems

Among multiple problems are the technical ones of who does the rating and how you design the forms. It is easy to measure how many managers have conducted an appraisal, but not so easy to measure how skilfully it has been carried out or its impact on the person appraised. When asked to rate ourselves, we will normally give ourselves a glowing review. At one conference, this time of coaches, the presenter asked the audience to shut their eyes and then raise their hands if they thought their own performance was outstanding. Almost every hand in the room went up, supporting research suggesting that the great majority of us believe we are at the 80th percentile when compared with other people – something that is statistically impossible. Self-appraisal is now a part of many such systems, but often this merely reveals the gap between appraiser and appraisee, resulting in many hours of bad-tempered emailed exchanges and squabbles over exactly which words will go into the final document.

Other frequent problems include a focus on the past, the one-sided (i.e. boss-led) nature of most appraisal discussions, the use of vague labels to describe behaviour, and the second-hand nature of much of what is offered as 'evidence'. It is also common for the appraisee to hear a negative criticism for the first time during the appraisal process.

This would matter less if there was proof that appraisals actually had a positive impact on performance, but the evidence points to it either having no impact or a negative one. Survey after survey shows that most employees see appraisal as an annoying box-ticking process that has nothing to do with their real work. This is particularly true when the organization applies the metrics of a so-called Bell Curve ('normal distribution'), thus rigidly determining that a pre-ordained percentage of employees must be judged (1) *super-wonderful*, (2) *pretty good*, (3) *okay*, (4) *problematical* or (5) *destined for the sack*. (The actual words are normally more nuanced than this but that is what they mean.) However skilful, subtly written, and politely discussed the rest of the process, none of it matters compared with the crude numerical summary conveyed by this final judgement. As a dismayed coaching client said, incredulity still in his voice, 'My whole work for the year reduced to a single number? Are they crazy?'

One study of 200 human resources professionals showed that such systems result in reduced productivity, cynicism, and damage to teamwork, create poor morale and a lack of faith in leadership. The essence of how to manage performance, a skill every boss needs to have, is not to rely on appraisal but to be able to build the kind of trust where honesty, mutual respect, and constant two-way feedback is at its core, something that is also at the heart of a coaching relationship.

Assumption: People can be managed through a carrot and stick approach

Early twentieth-century experiments on animals showed that you could shape behaviour by what you rewarded or punished. The carrot-and-stick metaphor comes from donkeys, beasts with legendary reluctance to do anything unless rewarded (carrot) or punished (stick). But human beings are not donkeys. We are not so easily manipulated. To understand this you need to look at the differences between extrinsic and intrinsic motivation, one of the most studied topics in sixty years of psychological research.

Extrinsic motivation is created by offering rewards such as money, status, cars, praise from others, prizes or those pleasant corner offices with two sets of windows. In other words, it is about reward that comes from external sources.

Intrinsic motivation is about what comes from inside: the feeling of being in control, of doing something that matters with meaning beyond mere self-interest, and of using our skills to their maximum. It is about our need for achievement, relying on our own judgement rather than on the judgement of others.

Study after study shows that intrinsic motivators are many times more powerful than extrinsic ones. Yet organizations consistently act on the opposite assumption – that it is extrinsic motivators that will reliably increase motivation. It is true that giving people extra money for trying extra hard can drive performance in some circumstances, but these circumstances turn out to be rather limited. Money works as an incentive only when the task is simple with straightforward solutions and one right answer. Where you need complex judgements and subtle thinking, financial incentives reduce rather than enhance performance. In fact, many studies have shown that the higher the financial rewards, the worse the organization's performance. A comprehensive chapter in Jeffrey Pfeffer and Robert Sutton's excellent book *Hard Facts, Dangerous Half-Truths & Total Nonsense* (2006) concluded that financial incentives 'damage performance with alarming frequency'.[2] First, they may attract the wrong sort of people – that is, people who 'come for the money, leave for the money'. Then, staff can get to expect bonuses as routine: in such cases we would expect the incentive effect to be minimal. Finally, it is often totally unclear on what grounds a bonus has been paid. The general effect of financial incentives is that they diminish performance and destroy teamwork while creating cynicism and mistrust of leadership.

Punishment

Punishment is equally ineffective. Think back to being punished as a child. How many people can remember what it was that they actually did to warrant the punishment? Mostly what we remember is the humiliation, indignation, and fear that the punishment evoked. When someone criticizes us, the instant response is to reject it. It offends our sense of ourselves as competent people, so the instinct is to brush it aside as unimportant. There can sometimes be a strong wish to punish in return. The feedback-giver is 'wrong' – they have failed to understand, they have a personal grudge. The most likely effect on behaviour is simply to put more effort into avoiding being caught another time. The uselessness of punishment can be seen at its most obvious in the criminal justice system. Seventy per cent of prisoners reoffend, so custodial sentences do not appear to deter or reform.

Praise

'Catch them doing something right' has been a popular variant on the carrot theme, in other words give people constant praise as a reward. But research shows that praise is not the all-purpose solution that you might assume. One well-known study carried out at Stanford University by Carol Dweck (2006) looked at the effect of praise on children. The results suggest that too much vague praise for being 'good' or for being 'clever' can have a counter-productive effect, creating caution, rigidity, and a fear of falling away from high standards. Skilfully and sparsely offered praise for *effort* and *method* was far more motivating. Other studies have shown that praise is a currency whose value drops the more frequently it is used, and that whether or not the recipient takes it seriously depends on their respect for the praise-giver and on how sincere they believe the praise to be.

The impact of all of this is often hard to see in the short term. If you reward with money or punish with negative comment, it may look as if your tactics have worked. There may be a mask of good behaviour and compliance, but in the long term, who knows what might be going on for that person?

The impact on managers

It has probably always been tricky to be a boss. But it is even trickier now, made more challenging by rapid social, techno-logical, and economic change. There is no longer any auto-matic respect for hierarchical authority; moral authority is the only kind that counts, and this has to be earned. Today it is much harder to hide, however rich, senior or famous you are. Indiscreet emails can be leaked by hostile colleagues, indiscreet behaviour can be spotted and videoed on the mobile phone of any passing onlooker. Disgruntled customers have blogs or websites where they can post comments that fight back against poor service.

The effects of severe recession can now be added to this mix. This has meant reducing costs, which usually means reducing staff. As coaches and consultants we have seen how this can directly affect our clients. For instance, some senior people have been the focus of hostile press articles that openly question whether they deserve their salaries. One such client found herself the target of abusive shouting in her local supermarket as a result. Another, forced by government policy to make savage cuts in headcount, was barricaded into his office for three hours by angry staff. Yet another was secretly filmed at a private staff meeting where he was explaining his policies. The recording was then digitally manipulated to make him look an idiot before being uploaded on YouTube.

Impact on behaviour

When you combine the influences of present-day economic difficulties with old assumptions about how to manage people, the impact on behaviour is considerable. The following are all common responses:

Fear, fear, and more fear. Fear often makes us behave badly and there is a lot of fear in organizations. Looking out for yourself can then be the first rule: hide, keep your head down. Fear of making mistakes and getting blamed is pervasive, even if, as the last person in the chain, there was little that you could have done to avert whatever calamity followed a mistake. Alibi emails, defensive politicking, secret meetings, moaning in corridors while pretending to agree with bosses in public, these are just some of the ways that people try to defend themselves.

Fear of delegating. Fear is contagious. If you believe your superiors will criticize you, you might think it easier to do a task yourself rather than delegate to someone. Thus you are at risk of doing other people's jobs as well as your own, leading to phenomenally long days and weekend working. In practice, what can happen is that bosses typically neglect their own proper jobs because they prioritize doing the work of their juniors. In some organizations, managers at every single level can be working one step below their true responsibilities, leaving the organization critically exposed because no-one is doing the strategic thinking that should be creating policy and guiding behaviour. Working at this level of intensity is not sensible or sustainable. Burn-out or rust-out will follow at some point.

Pointless meetings. When the organization is webbed with fear or with beliefs that people higher up know best and know more, meetings become more frequent, longer, with more and more attendees, each of whom has to have their say and none of whom truly listens to what anyone else is saying. As one of our clients said dryly, relief in her voice at having finally decided to leave, 'I got fed up with so very many meetings, so very many big tables, and so very many small minds . . .'.

Front line and junior staff who know 'the truth' but remain unheard. Front line staff usually do know what is going on because they are directly facing customers. In many organizations, there is a disconnect between what these staff know and what senior managers believe to be happening. When an organization slides into bankruptcy, it is rarely a surprise to the front line. Fear of being punished as bearers of bad news is at least one of the reasons why these messages do not percolate into the boardroom. When more junior people see that something is wrong, it is hard to speak up, or when you do, to be taken seriously. Spectacular twentieth and twenty-first century disasters of organization life include: the *Challenger* tragedy; the explosion at Three Mile Island; the *Exxon Valdez* oil spill; the banking crisis; the many serious railway and shipping accidents; inexcusable failures at NHS hospitals. All of these could have been averted if subordinates who knew what was likely to happen – and were right – had been able to insist on being heard.

Demotivated staff. Using your innate talents and continuing to develop involves having responsibility and taking risks, especially the risks of getting something wrong. Denying people the opportunity to do this is profoundly undermining. It creates under-confident, grumpy, and disengaged staff. They learn that you don't trust them. They learn that you prefer to do things yourself because you believe they can't. Disengaged staff create mischief.

Decision bottlenecks and an overstretched senior team. Fear means people are afraid of making decisions so they become expert at delegating upwards. So the most senior teams may be as much victims of all of this as anyone else. Their much higher salaries do not compensate for what they give up. They have to make too many decisions, do too much of the thinking, do too much work generally, relentlessly surrendering their leisure time and often sacrificing their health as well.

Healthy counter-influences

From the 1940s onwards, challenges to all of these deeply rooted assumptions began to arise. Kurt Lewin, a refugee from Nazi Germany, conducted action research into leadership demonstrating in experiments that have been repeated many times since with the same results, that authoritarian leadership produces apparent short-term compliance but soon creates fighting back, sabotage, and poor results; that *laissez-faire* leadership which is timid and over-consensual merely creates tensions around who is in charge and that these distract from performance. Lewin showed that the only leadership that produces both committed participants and impressive bottom line results is what he called *democratic* – where there is an emphasis on goals, feedback, and participation.

The importance of understanding and respecting customers and of involving rank-and-file staff in the business followed the enormous success of Tom Peters and Robert Waterman's book *In Search of Excellence*, first published in 1982. One of Peters' avowed aims was 'to challenge the influence of the bean counters'. The triumphs of Japanese manufacturing encouraged the Total Quality Management (TQM) movement. TQM can only work through the active participation of the workforce. Peter Senge's influential book *The Fifth Discipline* (1990) made the case, both in human and business terms, for individuals and organizations to go on learning. Stephen Covey's bestseller *The Seven Habits of Highly Effective People* (1989) stressed the need to look again at assumptions about leadership and its essential accompaniment, followership, pointing out that without the ability to influence others skilfully, any leader will be lost. For a while in the 1990s, 'empowerment' was a popular theme, alas often undermined when organizations, with no noticeable sense of irony, *ordered* their people to be *empowered*. Daniel Goleman's work (1995) on emotional intelligence has filtered into virtually all management and leadership development courses. These ideas have had an impact: the case for cooperation, collaboration, practising what you preach, and participation, all have usefully softened the influences of Taylorism.

The emergence of coaching

Coaching itself, the focus of this book, emerged from the 'human potential movement' which began in California in the late 1960s and from the rise of forms of therapy which assumed, as did the adherents of the human potential movement, that human beings are infinitely resourceful and have an innate drive to personal growth; we are responsible for ourselves and can achieve our potential without exploiting or manipulating others. *Coaching*, in the sense that we use the word now, began in the 1980s as a service offered by external professionals, often from a therapy, occupational psychology or training background, to the most senior managers in organizations. It was so successful that organizations frequently recruited and trained internal cohorts of people who had day jobs alongside their duties as volunteer coaches. When this, too, was successful, it became clear how powerful coaching would be as an approach to line management generally.

Summary

So we come back to the central paradox. You have to manage performance and hold people to account because that is what it means to be a manager. At the same time, you can no longer order people about: they resist and in any case ordering people about no longer works, if it ever did. Myths and half-truths pervade management thinking, whether it is the belief that you can motivate people through money, keep people's personal lives at bay, manage through rationality or that appraisal systems work as a way of managing performance. Mostly these beliefs result in precisely the opposite of what is intended. They waste time and energy, create fear and dependency, and deprive organizations of the creative energy that is critical to survival, especially at a time of economic crisis when the role of manager is under pressure and scrutiny as never before. Learning how to resolve these challenges by using what is firmly rooted in evidence and in an understanding of how human psychology really works is the topic of this book.

Coaching as the centrepiece of your approach to management is a key part of the solution and in Chapter 2 we look at the evidence and ideas that link high levels of employee motivation with high levels of organization performance and with coaching as a simple and effective way of creating both.

Notes

1. http://www.newyorker.com/reporting/2011/05/16/110516fa_fact_lane#ixzz1XON5UGeS
2. For an entertaining and authoritative summary of the research on financial incentives generally, take a look at Dan Pink's presentation on TED.com.

2 HOW COACHING SOLVES SO MANY MANAGEMENT PROBLEMS

In this chapter, we look at how and why coaching can solve so many of a manager's typical problems. We write from research-based evidence, and from hard practical experience, not myth or wishful thinking. Essentially, our case here is that a coaching approach is closely aligned with creating *employee engagement* (the current phrase for high levels of employee commitment and motivation), in itself shown repeatedly to correlate with outstanding bottom line performance.

The link between coaching and employee engagement

A young friend, lolling about for a few weeks while waiting to go to university, was kindly driving one of us (Jenny) to a large and well-known organization where she had a meeting with a senior manager. Instructed to wait and to buy himself a cup of coffee in the grandiose foyer, he had nothing to do but amuse himself by observing the people. As Jenny emerged from the meeting, he said, 'Jenny, why does everyone here look so miserable? They walk in all hunched up, lots of them are scowling, they're not talking to each other. And why are there so many CCTV cameras and security people? This isn't MI5!'

He had spoken naively but more truly than he knew. This organization had fiendishly deep-rooted problems. It had a culture of obsessive secrecy, poor staff–management relationships, terrible morale, and rapidly declining performance, the superficial symptoms of which were evidently all too visible, even to a passing eighteen-year-old. We contrast this with a visit to the Virgin Atlantic HQ building where a similar area was abuzz with cheerful people dressed in bright colours, had a desk where a smiley personal trainer was available for bookings, and there was a relaxed but businesslike atmosphere.

What does every boss want from his or her staff? There's no mystery about the answer: people who will work hard, work willingly, be loyal and discreet, open to learning, good humoured, never whine or say things behind your back that they will not say to your face. This ideal employee is positively involved with their job and with the organization. He or she passionately believes in the purpose of the organization and believes that his or her own work adds value.

In the language of management gurus, this is *employee engagement*, and it is more than just 'job satisfaction', being 'a learning organization', 'having a positive culture' or 'excellent morale'. It is about intensely felt individual attachment to the organization. People try harder, they are loyal to their colleagues, they feel ownership of the organization, and that they are working for the success of the entire enterprise.

Here are some small examples of how it works when you are on the receiving end as a customer:

- A young barista at a branch of Starbucks, faced with a disappointed five-year-old and his parents, phoned a neighbouring branch and sprinted the 500 metres there and back to obtain a gluten-free cake
- One of Vodafone's salespeople called back twice to check that a problematical new BlackBerry was now working properly
- A local pharmacist personally delivered, unasked, a packet of urgently needed drugs to a disabled patient who had forgotten to order his repeat prescription
- A heating engineer from British Gas stayed an extra two hours on a late Friday afternoon call-out in the middle of winter to make absolutely sure that a capricious boiler was now behaving itself
- Two nurses from the NHS Royal London Hospital travelled 200 miles on their day off to be at the funeral of a

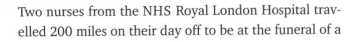

young patient and to support the parents they had come to know so well during the last month of her life

- A National Express employee at Stansted Airport organized a free bus ticket to London, plus cups of tea and tactfully offered company, for a distressed passenger whose wallet had been stolen.

These are small examples from our own experience. None of these employees needed to do what they did. They could all have shrugged their shoulders and expressed either polite negatives or indifference. You could say that these were all decent people and that their behaviour arose from deeply held moral values – and this is probably true. But it is highly likely that they behaved as they did because such values were explicitly endorsed in their organizations. Good customer care is more than being told to smile nicely. It can only truly happen consistently when people feel themselves well managed and when their bosses realize that management is a service whose customers are their own team members rather than believing that you have a divine right to order people about.

Here is how it sounds when employees feel engaged:

I have worked for XXXX (a well known consultancy and Think Tank) for two years. I have never known a place like it. I even look forward to Monday mornings! We are a tight-knit team of professionals and I learn something from my colleagues every day. If you make a mistake it's no big deal (though you wouldn't want to make the same one twice) and experiment is encouraged. I am only 28 and I have a lot of responsibility, it's very daunting sometimes, but I know I can and do ask my boss for help. She's a brilliant coach — never tells me what to do, but is very challenging and gets me to do the thinking. A lot of people who work here are quite eccentric but everyone knows they contribute hugely in terms of ideas. It must be working because we keep on getting interesting new contracts. There's a sense of playfulness in our meetings, which I love. When I hear people scoff at 'consultants' and how they cost the earth without adding value I am quick to defend my organization as the exception to the rule.

Research overwhelmingly shows that when you have employee engagement like this, a number of other highly desirable effects follow. Some of these are described, for instance, in Michael Treacy's book *Double Digit Growth* (2003). You retain the most talented people, people behave with more care about safety, you reduce sickness absence, increase productivity, and improve customer service. In fact, when you measure customer satisfaction and compare it with employee engagement in the same organization, the correlation is high, something that is potentially worth many millions of pounds in hard, bottom line profit. One large study across 26 countries and commissioned by the Gallup Organization[1] showed that organizations which score at the highest possible level of employee engagement perform nearly five times as well as those at the bottom.

How do you know if you've got engagement?

Definitions of employee engagement vary, but most have several elements in common. This is our own blend of many of the common factors that employees would describe if an organization had 'engagement' from its staff:

- Being treated as a whole human being, not just a work machine; having a boss who respects your feelings
- Taking the career development of employees seriously, even where there is little realistic chance of promotion because the hierarchy is so flat – in such cases, a boss might coach a person out of the organization, despite this being not in the immediate short-term interests of the boss
- Investing in the development of employees
- Designing jobs that allow people to use all their skills – and to acquire more through the stretch of delegation and of taking on new projects
- Being encouraged to suggest ideas for improvement of all sorts, even where these might seem irritating because they challenge the status quo
- Getting encouragement, feedback, and other forms of skilfully offered recognition
- Understanding where your job fits into the larger work of the organization; respecting its mission and purpose
- Being well informed and given accurate information about what is happening in the organization
- Believing that your job has meaning beyond just making money for you or for the organization
- Working in a team climate characterized by trust: mutual liking is only possible where this is the case.

The behaviour of your immediate boss is the most significant way of creating engagement and all of the factors above are opportunities for coaching.

Ask yourself how engaged you feel now in your own job by filling in the following brief questionnaire. We have marked with an asterisk the nine questions that are most directly linked with coaching behaviour by a boss; the remaining three are indirectly linked with boss behaviour.

	Yes ✓	No ✓
*My boss takes a keen interest in me as a human being		
*The organization invests in my learning and development		
My job is important		
*I am clear what is expected of me at work		
*I have helpful conversations about my future with my boss		
*I get a lot of recognition for my work		
*I ally myself closely with my colleagues		
*My ideas about how things can improve in the organization are taken seriously		
*I'm fully able to use my skills at work		
*I am developing in my role all the time		
I respect what this organization does		
I feel well informed about what is going on in the organization		
	High ✓	Low ✓
Your overall level of engagement?		

In relation to your own boss, what do you think he or she could improve?

Since what we experience as a subordinate has a major impact on how we behave ourselves as bosses, how many of these behaviours might apply to you?

The essence of employee engagement is that *staff try hard without being told to*. Scott Adams, the gifted cartoonist who created the anti-hero Dilbert, is, as ever, ready to satirize current buzz words in management. Recently, he had Dilbert's utterly incompetent nincompoop of a boss ('The Pointy Haired Boss') refer to employee engagement, stating, 'I don't know the details but it's something to do with you idiots working harder for the same pay'.

Theories X and Y: Do we have to be forced to work?

A distinguished mid-twentieth-century psychologist, Douglas McGregor (1960), identified two sets of beliefs underpinning how managers behave. Managers who espouse *Theory X* take a grim view of human nature. People are slackers who are out for themselves and work only for money; you need threats and coercion to make them do anything. You need a steeply hierarchical structure run by managers with narrow spans of control so that the boss can keep a close eye on underlings. Managers motivated by Theory X would totally understand Frederick Taylor's ideas (see p. 13). They shout, threaten, blame, confuse giving orders with delegating, over-supervise, are obsessive about detail, concentrate on cost-cutting to the detriment of quality, rarely praise or even thank people, and hug responsibility to themselves at the same time as making their staff accountable for anything that goes wrong.

You may think this too extreme to describe anyone's actual behaviour, but we have seen many examples of managers who do all of the above.

Marika was a middle manager in the finance function of a sales organization. Whistleblower complaints about her behaviour turned out to be well justified. But the point about Marika was that she sincerely believed herself to be the victim of her staff, the only one who truly cared about accuracy and quality. After a hard day's screaming (yes, really), shouting, nagging, exhorting, watching, and reproving to get her team to produce accurate management accounts, she went home exhausted, complaining of headaches brought on by overwork. 'I keep *telling* them to take responsibility', she said. 'Why won't they do it?' Out of Marika's small team of seven, six were applying for other jobs. The seventh was the whistleblower.

Or how about this? The scene is a meeting with some senior managers in an English local authority as a prelude to working with the executive team. In the middle of the meeting, a member of this team burst rudely into the room and delivered a loud telling off, shouting and ignoring the consultant, the guest – and a total stranger. He then stormed out again, banging the door so hard that the pictures rattled. The consultant was speechless and said to the interviewees, 'What happened? What was that about?' 'Don't worry' they said, 'he gets like that, we just try to ignore him'. Four months later this man went off sick with 'stress' and was absent for 12 months. It is safe to guess that his stress was entirely self-inflicted. Nothing about the way he managed people worked and he probably had no clue why.

Theory Y managers believe that people are motivated through wanting to do good work. They will blossom if you let them get on with their tasks with self-control. They come to work to do well and are essentially motivated, not by money, but by being able to participate, take responsibility, and exercise all of their innate skills. Most people can bring creativity to problem-solving as long as you give them the chance.

Research tells us that the behaviour you portray will trigger the behaviour you get in response. So managers who believe in Theory X will soon believe that their ideas are justified because as bosses, they will have to work harder and harder to make any impact on their teams with smaller and smaller results. If you believe in Theory Y, you will see people develop and grow.

What is coaching?

If only the word *coaching* did not have so many different meanings. Sports coaches may include those red-faced football managers who shout from the touchlines (though well-trained contemporary sports coaches would never, ever do this, as they know it is hopelessly ineffectual); maths coaches may coax your reluctant fifteen-year-old through GCSEs; and that's quite apart from new professions like executive coach or life coach. And where does the role of 'mentor' fit in? Is it the same as a personal trainer? Old professions have been repackaged in bright new coaching colours, so that a debt counsellor is now a debt coach, and spotted at an exhibition recently was a tarot love coach. No wonder the word is capable of so much misinterpretation when applied in a management context.

Here is our definition

> *Coaching is the art of facilitating another person's learning, development, and performance. It raises self-awareness and identifies choices. Through coaching, people are able to find their own solutions, develop their own skills, and*

change their own attitudes and behaviours. The whole aim of coaching is to close the gap between potential and performance.

The essence of coaching is that it encourages people to take responsibility for themselves, to experience themselves as powerful, to go on learning, to be creative in problem-solving, in charge of their own development, able to make excellent decisions, and to fulfil their potential. That we are born with the capacity to do this is the gift that evolution has bestowed on us. Advances in neuroscience prove that far from being fixed in youth and then destined to steady, tragic decline, our brains are 'plastic' and can continue to develop into old age. Yet it is clear how easily the human spirit can be crushed. We all know people who sit apathetic-ally in front of their TV screens, do little at work, dream away their time at school, engage in mindless activity involving alcohol or drugs, and then blame others when their lives take the wrong turnings. What decides which way it turns out? The answer is that our social environments are the critical factors, whether when growing up or in our work lives.

Formal and informal coaching

In this book, we are mostly describing *informal coaching* – that is, the kind of coaching that happens with little fanfare as part of a manager's day-to-day activities. In these conver-sations, it is unlikely that you will label them as such with any of your staff, regardless of how long or short they are and whether they are planned or spontaneous. We would distinguish this from *formal coaching*, which is what happens when you undertake a qualification such as those offered by the ILM, where the coaching needs to be planned, logged, and assessed. However, the essential skills are the same.

The importance of motivation

Everything is about motivation. Without motivation nothing will happen. Research (e.g. Ryan and Deci, 2000) shows that there are three factors that make all the difference:

- *Autonomy*: the belief that you can control your own life and having opportunities to do so
- *Relatedness*: feeling connected with others in a positive way that encourages trust and liking
- *Competence*: knowing that you have and use valuable skills, qualities, and abilities.

Coaching works because it is entirely based on psychologically proven principles: the more you encourage *autonomy*, *relatedness, and competence,* the more confident people will be and the better the work they will do. Everything a skilled coach does is permeated by keeping these needs in mind. The opposite is also true: the more you rob people of autonomy through excessive controls, neglect to create mutually positive relationships, and deny them opportunities to develop competence, the worse their performance will become. When you look at any failed human group, whether it is a family, an organization or a state, the ultimate reasons will be that these principles have been denied and severely compromised.

Coaching and other similar activities

Coaching is not the same as some other methods of developing people, though it shares a number of common strands with them. The following are the main differences:

Similar or related disciplines	Coaching
Therapy and counselling Assumes the person is ill and needs a 'cure'/help and has temporarily lost their sense of resourcefulness	Coaching assumes the person is well and can solve their own problems; typically has a strong focus on goals. It is 'work' rather than 'help'
Training Owned by the trainer; working to an external curriculum. The assumption is that knowledge will pass from trainer to trainee	Coaching is owned by the coachee; there is no external curriculum or timetable. The coach does not assume that he or she necessarily has knowledge that the coachee lacks
Mentoring Assumes the mentor is older, wiser, and knows best. A mentor offers trusted advice based on experience	Coaching assumes the coachee knows best. The coach rarely offers advice but encourages coachees to wrestle with problems themselves
Appraisal A formal part of the control system happening at infrequent intervals and is a judgement by the manager on the appraise	Coaching is an informal process of development that can happen every day; judgement on performance is only a small part of what takes place
All of the above Have a power differential: the therapist, trainer, mentor, and appraiser assume the more 'senior' role	Coaching is far more a relationship of equals: for purposes of the conversation, even where one person (the manager) is technically more senior than the other

Other distinctions

Line-manager coaching shares much in common with *executive coaching*. The difference is that an executive coach has no responsibility for the performance of the coachee. An executive coach may be an internal coach, someone who has a day job or even who fulfils this role full time and has been trained to coach colleagues where there is no line-management relationship or other conflict of interest. More often, executive coaches work independently and are paid for by the organization and hired as contractors, normally working with the most senior people in the organization. Their objectivity, knowledge of organization behaviour, and experience in other sectors gives remarkable freedom to challenge and support in equal measure. *Life coaches* focus on personal life dilemmas with secondary consideration for professional issues.

Coaching is now widely recognized as one of the most effective ways of developing people and a powerful approach to managing performance. Unlike training, which normally involves a group of people and is time-limited, coaching is a focused, one-to-one method that can happen any day, any time. As your coachee's line manager, you have daily opportunities to observe the person in action and endless chances to discuss their behaviour, working with them to fine-tune it where necessary. Unlike some forms of training, coaching is not a quick fix that is just as quickly forgotten. It is about sustainability and long-term impact on both the individual and the organization.

As a line-manager coach, your role is to work with your coachees to establish what they want to achieve, to nail whatever they believe is stopping them from achieving it, to identify the choices, and then to take action.

Coaching in action: An example

Carl works for a food technology company that specializes in flavourings for fast-food brands. He is a scientist by background and is in his first managerial role. Here is his account of how his behaviour changes as his understanding about coaching is revolutionized:

> I learnt about coaching on a course. Originally I was highly sceptical and I didn't want to spend time away from work. But I became a convert. Previously I thought I was already coaching my staff but when I remember what I did, the conversations would go a bit like this:

Team member	Can I have five minutes.
Me (*frowning*)	Of course, come in.
Team member	I've got this problem with the work we're doing for Betsy's Burgers. It's all coming in too expensive and I don't think the client will like the extra costs.
Me (*feeling annoyed and probably showing it*)	[Asks a few questions about the project, establishes the potential overspend] Yes, I don't think the client will like that, we need to find a way of reining in the costs.
Team member (*timidly*)	No, I know, that's why I thought you'd know what to do.
Me	Have you thought of [doing X]?
Team member	Oh no, I haven't – that's a good idea!

| Me | Or [Y] might also work. [Describes Y in some detail] |
| Team member (*exiting as quickly as possible*) | Great – I'll try those – thanks, Boss! |

I honestly thought this was coaching and that I was being helpful. I was certainly pleased with myself for generously granting the team member a few minutes of my time. In fact, after the training I quickly realized that what I was actually doing was undermining him because I had done every bit of the thinking and he'd done none. I hadn't really listened to him at all – I was too wrapped up in my own anxiety about the cost overrun and how this might reflect badly on me. I felt stressed and irritable because I didn't really want to be interrupted and it's exhausting thinking through other people's problems for them all the time. In my new guise as a manager-coach, I now assume that the team member is perfectly capable of thinking it through for themselves, so the conversation takes a different tack:

Team member	Can I have five minutes? Is now a good time?
Me (*smiling*)	Of course, come in.
Team member	I've got this problem with the work we're doing for Betsy's Burgers. It's all coming in too expensive and I don't think the client will like the extra costs.
Me (*patiently*)	Tell me where things currently stand . . .

Team member	[Describes the potential overspend; sounds alarmed]
Me (*calmly*)	You sound worried about this but I'm sure it's sortable. What help do you need from me in this conversation?
Team member (*hesitant*)	I've got a few ideas about what we might do, but I'm not sure whether they're go-ers or not.
Me	So – you need from me . . .?
Team member	Just discuss with me whether you think I'm on the right lines or not, then I can get on with it.
Me (*aware I need to summarize what he want*s)	So you'd like me to review your ideas with you?
Team member	Yes.
Me	OK – let's get into it: tell me what your thoughts are about how to solve it. What are the various options as you see them?

Essentially, this guy already knew the answers and all I did was ask at each stage, 'So what are the choices and what would be the pluses and minuses of each of those choices do you think?' Once he'd described them and we'd briefly discussed them, I said, 'OK so which do you think is the best option?' Actually, my own view was that there was nothing much to choose between them, so I just agreed that his choice was the one we'd follow. He left the room beaming and telling me he'd report back in two days. He did and he got the project back on track. The conversation did take longer – about twenty minutes instead of five, but what I noticed was that his confidence increased hugely and from that point on he began to come to me less and less on that kind of problem and only with the really major stuff, so in the long run I saved a huge amount of time.

Notice that the critical differences in Carl's accounts of the two conversations are that first, he understood that it was not his role to solve the problem because the team member was perfectly capable of solving it himself, and that second, he asked the powerful question, *What help do you need from me in this conversation?* This allowed the team member to set the goal for the discussion and then to take the major part in how it ran.

This is why the skills of line-management coaching are about creating empathy and trust, listening more than you talk, setting clear goals, asking powerful questions, giving and receiving feedback, and staying non-judgemental. This kind of conversation is rare, because as a boss it can feel as if there is enormous pressure to find the solutions for the people we manage. It can come from a genuine desire to help, but it is help of an unhelpful kind, leading to unconfident staff, too timid to think for themselves. It results in managers who are doing too much of the work of their team members as well as desperately trying to find the time to do their own.

Never underestimate the impact coaching can have on the coachee. This client describes how coaching from a skilled boss has helped. She describes the very common situation of having less self-confidence than it might appear on the surface, especially in unfamiliar settings such as external meetings.

People would probably think of me as being pretty confident, outgoing, happy to talk about anything at anytime to anyone; but actually that's not really me. To give a simple example, my boss coached me about ways in which it's possible to make a constructive contribution to a meeting when you know very little about the subject matter and you know the other people attending even less. When you go to meetings, you often know at least some of the people or you'll know something about some of the topics being discussed. You've got confidence based on personal knowledge – knowledge of the people or knowledge of the subject matter. Through coaching I learnt how to ask constructive and intelligent questions as a way of making an effective contribution to such meetings in a relatively easy way. This is not as easy for many people as it may look and coaching was hugely helpful for me.

The differences between traditional managers and managers as coaches

There are considerable differences in beliefs and behaviours between a manager acting from traditional principles and one operating from a coaching perspective. When you operate out of a coaching perspective you believe in people's resourcefulness. You no longer feel you have to know everything, have to keep a firm grip on events, or be ever vigilant for mistakes, nor will you find it hard to say, 'I don't know', or, 'I got that wrong'. Believing you have to control everything is intrinsically stressful because it is impossible and there will be literally no limits to the dangers you feel you must look out for. The well-worn cliché of *plate-spinning* is all too accurate. The plate-spinner can never rest because unless the plates are constantly watched and touched, they will fall. The coaching manager asks, 'What do *we as a team* need to do to be successful?' rather than 'How can I set up a system that allows me to control everything?' The typical skills and behaviours will put the emphasis in a different place. The following table sums up the differences.

	Traditional manager	Manager as coach
Beliefs about my role	• Power comes with the job • More seniority means more stress • Decisiveness is important • I protect my staff by telling them what to do • I add value by giving direction	• I have to earn authority • Sharing responsibility reduces stress • My staff are intrinsically resourceful • I encourage prudent risk-taking • I add value by developing my people
I am good at	• giving instructions • clarifying and analysing problems • making decisions quickly • offering people my solutions • creating momentum and urgency	• listening without judging too soon • facilitating other people's thinking • challenging people's self-imposed barriers • offering feedback • holding people accountable for jointly made decisions
I dread	• my staff getting something wrong • expressing uncertainty • admitting mistakes	• avoiding opportunities for feedback • undermining my staff by doing their thinking for them • showing off how experienced I am
Enjoyment in my role comes from	• pleasure in my status and its tangible rewards	• seeing my staff develop

This is not to say that there is no place for traditional behaviours, beliefs, and principles because there is. In a crisis, you need leaders who are able to act decisively. There will be occasions and contexts where the superior experience of the boss needs to hold sway. It is not always appropriate to consult and coach, nor is there anything intrinsically wrong in enjoying the tangible rewards of a more senior role.

Coaching is not abdication or a soft option

Coaching is the opposite of abdicating your responsibility as a boss. You are clear at all times that your coachee reports to you and that you are jointly responsible for what is achieved. You are encouraging the coachee to think for him or herself but you are not surrendering accountability. Nor is coaching a soft option. In fact, for a so-called 'soft' skill, it can take hard effort to learn and persistence to apply.

Summary

Employee engagement is what every manager wants from their teams. Engagement means a fierce individual loyalty to the organization, its mission and purpose, feeling that you are contributing ideas and skills, seeing where your own job fits in, and being willing to make significantly more effort to satisfy the needs of customers than is strictly necessary. Our natural instincts are towards the self-fulfilment that satisfies our needs for freedom to think and act for ourselves, warmth and connectedness with others, and the opportunity to develop competence. By practising coaching as the way to achieve all of this, a manager can facilitate the team member's learning and release much-needed time for getting on with his or her own job. When engaged in this way, people work hard without being prodded. The evidence shows strong and direct links between this behaviour and bottom line success.

Coaching works as a way of creating engagement because it links to everything we know about what motivates us to work.

If all this sounds desirable, then it is worth learning how to do it. In the next chapter, we look at some fundamentals about coaching, the most fundamental of which is the principle of choice: that we choose how we respond to even the most overwhelming of challenges and that giving advice is usually counter-productive.

Note

1. Go to www.gallup.com and search Meta-Analysis: The Relationship Between Engagement at Work and Organizational Outcomes for a PDF version of their report.

3

THE COACHING MINDSET

In this chapter, we describe the operating principles and mindset that you need to be a brilliant line-manager coach. We explain the principle of choice that underlies all human behaviour, even when we believe we can do 'nothing', because *doing nothing* is in itself a choice. We show the importance for any coach of listening out for the irrational beliefs that limit people. We describe how giving a team member well-meant advice in the guise of 'coaching' is normally counter-productive.

We all choose how we feel and behave

It may seem obvious that we all choose how we feel and behave, but in practice we often talk as if is not true. Take your teenage son who has left his school blazer on the bus. Trying hard to manage your annoyance, you ask how this could have happened. 'Mr Green kept me behind for talking in the lesson, the others talked just as much but didn't get the blame, then Tracey tried to snatch my bag and my blazer got left behind'. Hmm. So it was Mr. Green and Tracey: nothing to do with the owner of the blazer? Most human beings are capable of thinking and talking as follows:

She made me do it.

When you talk to me like that it makes me feel as if I'm a failure.

I can't help how I feel, it's just how I am.

Everyone else is doing it, so why shouldn't I?

It's your fault, if you were a better boss I'd be better at what I do.

The government takes so much of my pay in taxes – I don't see why I should work hard.

If you hadn't forced me to take that job, I'd still be in my old one and I'd be so much happier.

No one else goes home before six o'clock, so I have to stay too.

No one ever gets fired here, so I can't tackle poor performance – HR won't support me.

What all the above statements have in common is that they put the responsibility on some outside agency: another person, the circumstances, the organization, the government or some mysterious quirk of our personality or temperament. Essentially we are trying to make others responsible for our happiness. This is impossible. No one else can 'make' you happy or unhappy, stressed or relaxed, miserable or ecstatically joyful. When we talk like this, the assumption is that how we respond to an event or to the behaviour of another person is not within our control. Actually, all of it is, and as a coach to your staff, one of your first tasks is to accept the principle of choice and to work with them to do the same. We choose our responses to whatever life throws our way – we always have and we always will. Furthermore, psychological health is strongly associated with being able to assume responsibility for oneself. It is the way we grow and develop. Try this little experiment now. Think of something you have told yourself you 'have' to do. Now try reframing this thought as 'I have chosen to . . .'. How different does it feel?

Alexi is a middle manager in a hotel chain. He is intelligent, conscientious, hard working and likeable. But there are certain situations where he flies into a rage. These all have to do with members of his team who make what he considers to be 'stupid mistakes' with guests. The last time this happened it was in full sight of the hotel's reception desk and the staff member concerned burst into tears and ran off as several transfixed guests looked on. Alexi was remorseful, as he always is, but when tackled by his boss, his excuse is that 'it's my fiery Russian temperament. All the men in my family are like this'. Alexi's boss has to coach Alexi into understanding that such behaviour is career limiting, and that it is entirely within his own gift to behave differently.

As a coach, your goal is to raise the awareness of your coachee that, like Alexi, we make choices all the time, whether we are aware of it or not. While it is true that we cannot magic away the feelings themselves because they come from a part of the brain (the limbic system) that is out of our conscious awareness, it is not true that we cannot control how we express them. It is only when we accept this and become conscious of that nanosecond of choice that we can make better ones.

This is how we will describe our emotional reactions in situations where we have behaved impulsively. The response has felt as if it has a life of its own. Thought has apparently not come into it – and indeed it has not.

Stimulus ⇨ Response

A better way of functioning is as follows, all of which can happen in a few microseconds:

Stimulus ⇨ Thinking ⇨ Decision ⇨ Response

Refusing to take responsibility can seem seductive and there can apparently be payoffs. As Homer Simpson, the much put-upon hero of the cartoon series once commented, 'You tried your best and you failed miserably. The lesson is, never try'. Here are some examples.

Avoiding the consequences of choice		Payoff
It's because I'm a woman; sexism is everywhere. If I were a man I'd have got further	so	I avoid looking at how my own behaviour may have contributed to my career problems
I could have succeeded if I'd tried hard	so	I never have to face up to the possibility that I might have failed anyway
You made me cry	so	it's all your fault and I avoid looking at how I contributed to the problem between us
You never take me seriously	so	I may be able to manipulate you by making you feel guilty

In the long term the payoff is worthless because it leads to feelings of perpetual powerlessness, to avoiding risk, to never speaking up or asking for what you want: the opposite of what you need any member of your team to be. It is extremely difficult to coach people who become addicted to the role of victim, but we offer some ideas about this on p. 189.

Uncovering hidden beliefs

Coaching is not just a simple matter of asking the coachee what they would like to do and then encouraging them to do it. What usually gets in the way is the beliefs we hold about ourselves and others. A belief is a principle accepted as true or real without proof. It represents thoughts and ideas we do no longer question. Whereas you can actually observe behaviour, you cannot observe beliefs, and when we think we know what beliefs another person holds, we may well be wrong, as beliefs are invisible.

The reason this is important is that beliefs have profound effects on our behaviour.

Aisha and Tasia are 26-year-old twins who have lived all their lives in London. Both have degrees from the same university. They are not identical even though they look similar. Their mother is Irish and their father is from an Afro-Caribbean background. Aisha is outgoing and optimistic and works as junior manager for a multi-national oil company in central London. She refers to herself cheerfully as a Brown-Skinned True Londoner, equally able to draw on her Irish and Afro-Caribbean origins and London upbringing, seeing it as a plus to have this triple heritage. She is taking full advantage of the development opportunities her company provides and has recently completed her first management course. She believes her future is bright and, encouraged by some coaching from her boss, will shortly be applying for promotion. She sees this as indicating to her employer that she is ambitious but she is realistic about the chances of her being successful. However, she is in it for the long haul, will prepare hard for the interview, and will not be too disappointed if luck doesn't go her way this time.

Tasia thinks of herself as Black. After almost a year of unemployment she has found a job as an Admin

---

Assistant in a local authority and feels gloomily certain that the job has no career prospects. She believes it is far more difficult for a black person to advance in British society because there is widespread discrimination and she can point to innumerable occasions where she has experienced it. She believes that it is more difficult for women to get promoted. She has refused to join the Black and Minority Ethnic group at work because she thinks it is 'just pointless talking'. Her boss is exasperated by Tasia's reluctance to attend team 'awaydays'. When he asks her why this is, she says dolefully, 'It's too stressful. Other people have got much better ideas and I'm afraid I'll look stupid'.

It is safe to forecast that while Aisha will do well in her career, Tasia's will remain stuck – unless she is lucky enough to encounter a boss who can challenge her deeply rooted belief that there is no point in trying because she will fail and that her mixed-race background is a hurdle she cannot cross. These two young women demonstrate that our beliefs have enormous effects, positive or negative, on our behaviour. As the saying has it, if you expect to succeed, you will and if you expect to fail, you will be right.

Figure 3.1 shows how it happens.

As a coach, one of your tasks is to listen out for beliefs. Often these will take the form of negative inner voices, all of them about fear of one kind or another:

People like me can't . . .

They'd laugh at me if I . . .

Be seen and not heard is my motto.

If I tried I might fail.

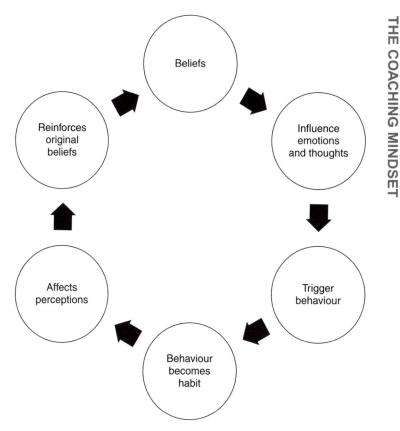

Figure 3.1 How beliefs affect behaviour

It's not my place to . . .

Other people are cleverer than me.

Other beliefs may take the form of flawed thinking, such as:

Things and people are black or white, good or bad.

Other people should look after me.

It's not fair.

My life should be easier than it is.

I must do everything perfectly or else it's not worth doing.

It's all my fault: I can never do anything right.

I must always put others first: my needs don't matter.

Never ask for help: be strong.

The point about these beliefs is that they are irrational if we apply them wholesale. There will be little or no evidence for them, yet we may behave as if they are a general rule of life and they become true because the behaviour we do triggers a predictable response from others. For example, if you believe that you will experience discrimination if you apply for promotion, you will probably not apply, and therefore your belief will appear to be justified.

How to tackle limiting beliefs

- The first step is to listen for signs that your coachee is being held back by a self-limiting belief. For instance, you can ask any of the following questions:

  So what assumptions are you making here?

  It sounds to me as if you are applying a personal rule-of-thumb here. I'm hearing you talk as if [*you name what you think the assumption or 'rule' might be*]. Is that right?

  So you say you want to do X [*e.g. make some change in behaviour*] but it's too difficult. What's holding you back?

- Then ask the coachee, 'What actual evidence is there that this is true?' Usually there will be very little and being able to explore this with a non-judgemental person may be the first step in breaking through the self-imposed barrier.
- Suggest designing a limited experiment to test the assumption, just to see what might happen.

Here is how one manager did this with a member of her team:

Michael is an intellectually gifted and experienced librarian and has just been promoted. His boss, the Chief Librarian, wants him to take a much more prominent part in team meetings, especially those where acquisitions policy is being developed, as she knows that Michael has strong opinions on the topic. But at meetings Michael either speaks in such a soft voice that people don't notice he is trying to get into the discussion, or is totally mute. This behaviour has annoyed some of his colleagues, one or two of whom believe he is being silent because he thinks he is 'too good for this team'. Having opened up the topic, Michael's boss challenges him hard by asking him one of the most powerful coaching questions of all: *What will happen if you do nothing about this?* Michael has to agree that the situation can only get worse and that his influence will decline – something he most definitely does not want to happen.

Boss	So I can see you don't like the idea that your colleagues think you're snooty.
Michael (*indignantly*)	No – because I'm not.
Boss	And you said you'd like to say more at the meetings. I'd like you to say more! So what's getting in the way?
Michael	They all talk so much I can't get in.
Boss	Oh come on . . . You could get in if you wanted to. What's this about for you?

[Long pause]

Michael (*reluctantly, blushing a little*)	I'm afraid that what I've got to say isn't up to standard – they're all so clever – and brash and noisy. And sometimes I start to speak and they just talk over me.
Boss	That's because you speak so quietly! What's the evidence that they're cleverer than you?
Michael	Well . . . Um . . . Er . . . Maybe it's just an impression and there isn't any now I come to think of it, but I've often thought that maybe I'm not as clever as other people think I am.
Boss	Michael, here's my challenge. At the next departmental meeting, I challenge you to speak three times using a much louder voice than your normal whisper and just see what happens. It doesn't matter whether it 'works' or not or what you actually say, it can be garbled nonsense if you like, or how the others react. Just notice what it feels like to join in. We'll discuss it at our next one-to-one.

Michael reluctantly accepted this challenge. To his amazement, his contributions, which he had thought lame and stumbling, and had made only with difficulty, had a dramatic effect. People came up to him after the meeting smiling and saying 'Those were good points'. Complicit in winking at him as they were leaving the room, the boss said, 'So it works, eh?'

It's not about giving advice

Most of the managers we train as coaches are deeply committed to doing a good job. They are conscientious and hard working. Typically, they have had a career-long commitment to analysing problems and this can often mean that they believe their role is to solve problems for their staff. The biggest single challenge that such managers encounter in learning how to coach is in giving up the idea that they are 'helping' by offering well-meant advice. In some cases, advice-giving is about rescuing – saving people from the disastrous results of their own dithering when, if given the chance – and some coaching – they could do whatever it is perfectly well.

Insistence meets resistance

Even when the advice we are given is entirely benign, or when we respond to a direct request to offer it, plus we know it's for our own good and the person offering the advice means the very best for us, our instinct is to resist (see Figure 3.2).

Being told what to do: a negative cycle

Think about any habit you have which is generally considered to be unwise: it could be smoking, driving too fast, drinking more than is good for you, taking too little exercise, eating too much or too little. The moment anyone offers you advice, we guarantee that your instinct will be resistance. When offered advice, the immediate human instinct is to feel some or all of these responses:

● *Indignation*: What does he or she know about me and my problem?

- *Anger and resentment*: It's all very well for him or her . . .
- *Feeling diminished*: How come I can't work this out on my own?
- *Fear*: They're probably right but I can't deal with it now.
- *Guilt*: I shouldn't have this problem.
- *Holding back*: I can't admit how awful I feel.
- *Indifference*: I don't respect this person and don't care what they think; why should I do what they want?

The typical response to advice, which is only a gentler version of being ordered or told what to do, results in an early decision to stop listening and to play the *yes-but* game. *Yes, you're right, but I can't do it right now. Yes, but I haven't*

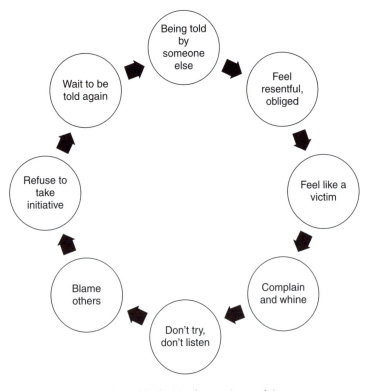

Figure 3.2 How being told what to do creates resistance

really got enough will-power. Yes, I know you're right (but actually I have no intention of doing anything about it). Biology as well as psychology is involved here. This is because the amygdala, the small almond-shaped part of your brain that acts as its alarm signal, hears the advice as an attack. The attack is on your sense of yourself as a competent and wise person and the other person is temporarily in the role of more competent and wiser person. Emotion takes over, your brain sends a flood of cortisol – a stress hormone – to your prefrontal cortex, the seat of rational thinking, and reduces its capacity to think. Because of this, it is likely that you will be unable to remember what the advice actually was. Cortisol helps if what you have to do is run away, but it is unhelpful if what you need to do is think clearly. The chances are that you will forget most of what you have been told. If you are told what to do and feel that you are obliged to do it, there are further negative consequences: resentment, feeling like a victim, being uncommitted to your actions, blaming others and then waiting sulkily to be 'told' all over again.

When we tell ourselves what to do, the results are very different. We take ownership, feel self-motivated and confident, seek to extend our influence, and offer ideas and solutions (see Figure 3.3).

Telling yourself what to do: a positive cycle

It is counter-productive to give advice. If people take it, you have undermined them by conveying that they were incapable of working out the answer for themselves. You are training them in helplessness and guaranteeing that you will have too much to do yourself, possibly neglecting your own job in order to demonstrate how well you can do theirs.

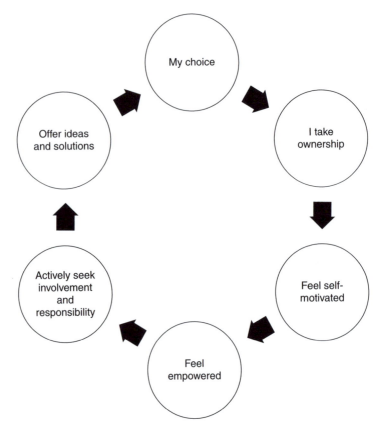

Figure 3.3 Deciding for yourself

What if the coachee actually asks for advice?

Charlie is an accountancy technician, struggling to fit the enormous amount of studying needed to complete a higher-level qualification with his full-time workload. The immediate problem is a piece of homework on tax law that is baffling him. He goes to his boss, a tax specialist, and says to her, *What's the answer? Advice please!* Julia could give him the answer in two minutes flat, and she is tempted to do so. It will give her the pleasant glow that results from helping someone younger and will reinforce her status as an expert. But she resists, knowing that if she does, Charlie will be trailing back to her office frequently and will be unlikely to find future answers for himself. So she ignores his request for 'the answer' and instead says, 'Tell me how you've tried to solve it so far'.

Charlie looks blank. The truth is that panic has overwhelmed him and the deadline for submission is tomorrow. Julia waits patiently. Charlie mumbles about his textbooks and on-line support group. 'So where might you look for the answer?'

The fog clears a little for Charlie. He realizes that Julia is not going to do the work for him. He remembers now that his tutor demonstrated a model answer to a similar problem in the last webinar.

Julia says, 'That sounds good to me. I know you can do this on your own Charlie, but come and tell me if you get stuck again'. Julia understands that Charlie is extremely unlikely to reappear in her office with this query.

Other tactics that work

- Just saying no: 'It's better if you work this out yourself, but I'll happily act as sounding board for you if you like'.
- Saying 'What would work for me is unlikely to work for you'.
- Explaining why you are not going to give advice but expressing your certainty that the person can find the answer themselves, then going straight to coaching questions using the OSCAR model (Chapter 6).

● Saying you will happily give your own view but *after* they have found their own solution.

When it's okay to give advice

You might be thinking that there must be many times when it is helpful to offer advice – for instance, that medical practitioners have to do it all the time because they have specialist knowledge that patients lack. True, but the evidence is that we patients frequently ignore our doctors' advice for all the reasons given above. At a minimum, 30 per cent of all prescriptions are never filled or the course of drugs is not finished and some studies have suggested that the proportion may be as high as 50 per cent. And in medicine, doctors are now increasingly being trained as coaches, where they find that working collaboratively with patients gets far better results: people are more likely to take their medication, feel more in control of their condition, and get better more quickly. This is proving to be true even when the patient's condition is chronic and has previously been resistant to treatment from a large number of medical practitioners. (For some examples, see p. 241.)

There is a place for advice in coaching but it's a much smaller one than many beginner-coaches realize. Only give advice if the answer to any one or more of these questions is yes:

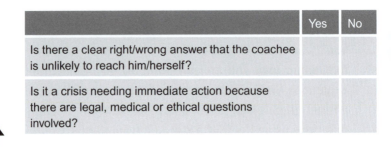

	Yes	No
Is there a clear right/wrong answer that the coachee is unlikely to reach him/herself?		
Is it a crisis needing immediate action because there are legal, medical or ethical questions involved?		

Is the coachee's wellbeing seriously at risk if you don't give them this advice?		
Are you offering facts, not opinions?		
Are you willing to suggest that the coachee questions the advice you offer – for example, asking, *That's my view, but how does it strike you*?		
Do you have deep expertise that the coachee is unlikely to be able to access in any other way?		
Is giving the advice unlikely to undermine the person or to create dependency?		
Are you sure that your own wish to offer the advice does not include any of the following: a wish to show off; wanting to emphasize that you have the power; can't be bothered to try coaching techniques?		

Offering information in coaching style

Instead of offering advice, it is better to consider that you may need to offer information, but there are still ways of doing this in coaching style. There will be many occasions as a boss when you have to give people information, and sometimes this is information that they will not want to hear. For instance:

- Giving someone bad news: they have not got the promotion they wanted, the department is to be downsized and their own job is at risk, a request for a pay rise has been rejected.
- The organization is to engage in a merger and this means a change to their job spec.
- They need to acquire new skills.
- A different IT system will be introduced.
- The physical layout of the office is to be changed.

Managers frequently struggle with how to convey these messages. 'I've told them time and again but it doesn't seem to sink in'. Is it possible to do this effectively and in coaching style? The answer is that it is certainly possible as long as you stick to a few simple principles.

First, remember that everything depends on rapport and on the relationship. The reason that people do not seem to take in difficult messages is that emotion gets in the way. If you are anxious yourself and dealing with an anxious person, the temptation can be to rush through your message, gabbling, using jargon with a 'phew, glad that's over with' sense of urgency. The trouble is that the other person does not actually have a hole in their heads into which you pour your information. They are not just a passive recipient but a human being and possibly someone with a lot at stake because of what you are trying to convey. They may be feeling bewildered, overwhelmed, worried, and preoccupied. There are several tactics that can help:

Asking permission

This may seem a bit disingenuous, since after all isn't it your job to tell people what to do? But asking permission makes a lot of difference because it creates a collaborative climate. It is the equivalent of giving a polite knock on someone's door before entering.

Andrew is a director at a garment factory that has just lost a lucrative contract with a British fashion retailer. The work is going to Turkey where costs are lower. The announcement has been made and now he has called in Becky to tell her what provision the company has decided it can make for the machinists in her department, many of whom will lose their jobs. After some brief pleasantries, he says, 'Becky, I've got some information to give you about what the Board has decided on redundancies. But first I'd like to check with you. Will it be best if I just outline the main points first, or would you like to hear the detail now?'

This has immediate impact on the discussion that follows. Being asked permission lowers resistance: it is courteous, it makes it more likely that the information will be heard. Becky's manner changes from sullen child to grown-up as she asks Andrew to give the headlines first. When Andrew asks permission it gives her back a little control in a situation where she has been feeling resentful and powerless.

Asking permission also works when you want to convey an idea of your own. So you might say

> *May I offer an idea here? My own experience is . . .*

or

> *May I make a suggestion?*

In this case, asking permission flags up that you are aware that your own idea is just one possible solution. You are deliberately diminishing the chances of the coachee interpreting it as an order.

Emphasizing the coachee's freedom to disagree

This may feel counter-intuitive. Do you really want to invite argument when maybe you are feeling uncomfortable yourself, especially if privately you do not endorse whatever policy you are discussing? But actually, by inviting disagreement you are merely acknowledging what is inevitable anyway – that people have their own views and that these may not coincide with yours.

> Further on into the conversation Andrew says, 'I'm aware you may not agree with this . . .'.
>
> And later still, he says, 'I guess you'll have your own views on this and I'd like to hear them, even though I'm afraid the policy can't be changed at this stage'.

Offering choices wherever possible

Even when there appears to be little room for manoeuvre, choices will be possible – at its simplest between doing nothing and doing something. Encouraging the other person to consider what the choices might be is yet another way of emphasizing autonomy. So your actual aim in the conversation might be to help the coachee make an informed choice.

> In the closing minutes of the discussion, Andrew turns to Becky's own situation. He says, 'It seems to me that you have several choices here. You could explore the option of moving to the Manchester factory where there will definitely be a job for someone with your skills and experience; you could apply for redundancy yourself; or you could stay on here and compete for one of the jobs that will be available after restructuring. But which of those seems to make most sense to you at the moment?'

Use the rhythm of draw out → provide information → draw out

This is an effective way of giving information and at the same time making beneficial change more likely. Instead of starting from your own agenda (*I need to give this person information and on my terms*), you start from theirs. So you might say,

> *What do you already know about this?*

or

> *Which aspect would it be most useful for us to concentrate on?*

This way you elicit from the other person what their interests and concerns are, answering and giving information on these as your priority rather than being preoccupied with what you need to tell them. The more you start from your own preoccupations, the lower your chances of influencing the other person. By starting in a different place, you accept the psychological reality of change. When hearing news of some major or minor organizational change, the human response is not, 'Oh, how interesting, I wonder what impact that will have on strategy?' Instead, it is always, 'How will this affect ME?' Essentially, you are providing information but then immediately encouraging the other person to voice his or her own interpretation using phrases like

> *What's your immediate response to this?*

> *How does that strike you?*

> *What are your feelings about this?*

Offer stories about how others have coped

This is a better way of offering helpful ideas than providing advice. By giving several anecdotes you will be suggesting that there is more than one approach to solving a problem and enabling yourself to stay neutral. It allows you to put the decision back in the coachee's court if, after describing ways that other people have found solutions, you say, 'All those approaches worked for them, but how does this strike you?'

Becky is anxious about how to cope with the anger of her factory floor staff, many of whom have blamed her for a decision in which she played no part, and one has even made vague threats of personal violence. 'What would you do?', asks Becky.

Andrew avoids the invitation to give advice. Instead, he says, 'Could I give you some examples of how other people have dealt with this?' [*asking permission*]. Becky nods. Andrew then gives her four brief stories of varying approaches that he has seen with colleagues, ending with, 'that's four quite dissimilar ways of tackling it. Which ones appeal to you?'

This is very different from falling into the advice trap and saying 'if I were you (*remember you never can be the other person*) I'd be firm and tell them their behaviour is unacceptable . . .'.

Five foundation principles of effective coaching

Our approach to coaching is underpinned by five foundation principles. Remembering and honouring them will help give shape and purpose to the coaching you do.

Principle 1: People are resourceful

They do not need to be fixed because they are not broken. The best answers are always the ones we give ourselves.

Principle 2: The coach's role is to increase the coachee's resourcefulness; it's not to give advice

The skill of coaching is in creating rapport, putting effort into understanding the coachee's perspective, raising their levels of awareness, setting clear goals for the conversation, asking questions, agreeing action, and reviewing the overall plan.

Principle 3: It's a collaborative relationship

When you are in the coaching role with a member of staff, you are equals for purposes of the conversation. This is the only way you will create the trust that is the foundation of effective coaching. The coachee has to be able to feel vulnerable with you – for instance, able to say that they are uncertain, fear making a mistake or don't know something they may feel they should know – without any dread of getting punished for their candour.

Principle 4: Take a whole-life approach

The evidence on the desirability of taking a whole-life approach is overwhelming. The more that staff are able to be frank with you about what is going on in their personal lives, the more seamless the connection between work and home, the easier and more enjoyable work becomes. The more you know about a coachee, the better equipped you will be to deal with whatever they bring you. Note that this does not mean that you should probe when people resist telling you about their private lives, or that you should try to be a counsellor or a marital expert, but it is important for a boss to know that a staff member may be struggling with troubles at home, with money problems or with a health problem that has become chronic and hard to manage.

Principle 5: Coaching is about change

If nothing needs to change, then people do not need coaching. As a line manager, the skill of coaching is identifying when change is needed, either because you spot it yourself or because a team member raises the topic. Part of your task here may be to raise the coachee's awareness that change is needed, for instance with feedback (p. 124). If people do not accept that they need to change, then coaching is impossible.

Summary

Coaching is underpinned by accepting the principle of choice. Life may throw unpleasant challenges our way but we always have the freedom to choose how we respond, even when under severe emotional pressure. Coaching is about making such choices explicit and raising the coachee's awareness of them. Advice undermines the recipient and the findings of neuroscience show that this is a biological as well as a psychological phenomenon, so there is a strictly limited number of times when it is useful to offer it. Even where your task is to offer information, some of which may be bad news for the recipient, the same values of collaboration and respect will apply. The foundation principles of coaching are to accept that the coachee is resourceful and that the role of the coach is to increase the other person's sense of their own resourcefulness, to act collaboratively, and to approach the coachee as a whole person rather than just as someone in whom your only interest is in their work. Coaching is always about change and if a coachee is reluctant to accept the need for change, coaching will not be the right option to take with them.

This is the coaching mindset, but mindset alone will not help you to coach effectively. The foundation skill is the skill of listening and we explain how and why this is so essential, as well as how to do it, in the next chapter.

4 BEING A BRILLIANT LISTENER

In this chapter, we explore the most fundamental coaching skill of all: listening. Listening is not the passive process it seems because it involves dedicated attention to the other person and exquisite attention to the language they are using. This skill is much taught on management development courses and, in our experience, practised rather rarely in real life.

Listening – that is, real listening

To be a brilliant line-manager coach you have to be a brilliant listener. Admitting that you might be less than perfect in this respect is a bit like owning up to having no sense of humour: uncommon. But how often in your life does someone really listen to you? *Really* listen? That is, without distracting themselves, without interrupting, without finishing your sentences for you, without any sense of hurrying you up or wanting to press their own ideas on you?

Unless you are an unusually lucky person, the chances are that you will rarely experience real listening. What most of us experience most of the time is pretend listening and sometimes not even that. While writing this chapter, we collected the following examples:

- Being told during a phone call, 'Go on, I'm listening', when the sounds of children being shushed and a dog shooed out of the way were all too obvious.
- The person at the other end of a phone line tapping away on their computer while saying distractedly, 'Mmm . . . yes . . . okay'.
- A doctor who kept his eyes on his computer throughout the consultation.
- Several people in a high-level meeting openly sending texts during the height of the discussion.

- A friend who cheerfully admitted to loading the dishwasher with the phone tucked between her ear and her shoulder during the conversation.
- A meeting where most of those attending just made speeches at each other and no one appeared to have listened to anyone else.
- A meeting in which a great deal of the time several people were talking at once and it was rare for anyone to be able to finish what they were saying without interruption.
- A sales assistant who kept up a brisk chatter with her colleagues during the transaction and communicated with the customer in sign language.
- Telling an acquaintance about a health scare only to have her interrupt with her own anecdote about a similar problem she had experienced.
- A cold caller from a telephone company insisting on ploughing on with his script despite clear signals that the call was unwelcome.

Being a successful coach means being able to listen with a much higher quality of attention than in these examples. When you can do this, you will be able to create a high level of rapport: the foundation of getting to the heart of what your coachee needs from you and creating the climate where they, in turn, will be willing to listen to you.

Rapport

Rapport means being genuinely connected to the other person. If you are not in rapport, trust will be absent, and in coaching everything is about trust. As the coachee, trust means being willing to make yourself vulnerable, to owning up to what you don't know, to expressing puzzlement and concerns. You will feel able to alert a boss to possible risks and failures, something that is hard to do when you suspect you will not be patiently heard out. Rapport is a consequence of authentic listening and this is a consequence of concentrating hard on the other person. It is a two-way process: you cannot 'do rapport' on your own. Rapport is a biological as well as a psychological phenomenon, an emotional rather than an intellectual process.

Outer signs of rapport

When you are in rapport, you may notice that you and the other person are in spookily matched postures. If you have one knee crossed, an arm thrown over the back of your chair, leaning forward or backward, the other person will soon be doing the same. As the other person shifts position, you find yourself giving a little shift too. As you scratch your nose, the other person will touch their face. Look at any pair of close friends in a pub and you will see this on show; for instance, each will lift their glass at precisely the same time.

Can you deliberately create rapport? Well, yes, up to a point. But if this becomes an exercise in mimicry beware, it will be fake rather than genuine rapport. Eventually, as one British politician said of another, renowned for his allegedly phoney smiles, you will look 'convincingly insincere'. Instead of consciously trying to copy the other person, we suggest that you monitor constantly how well you are actually matched, looking at factors such as posture, gesture, breathing, voice volume, speed and energy of speech. If you are not in rapport, you may see any of the following signs – and others like them:

- You are slumped in your chair but the coachee is leaning upright and forward
- You are speaking loudly, the coachee is whispering

- One of you constantly avoids eye contact
- The coachee is agitated and nervous, while you are calm
- You are speaking quickly and talking a lot, while the coachee is speaking slowly and talking very little – or vice versa
- One of you is fiddling with hair, necklace or watch while the other is still.

Notice these signs as symptoms – you are not in rapport – and ask yourself why. If the responsibility lies with the other person, then they are conveying their distraction. You cannot go on until you have inquired into it. So you might say

> *I notice you look a bit uncomfortable: what's going on for you?*

> *The energy seems to have gone out of you – you seem less animated than you were a moment ago.*

If the responsibility lies with you, then the most likely reason is that you have been unable for some reason to suspend judgement or to concentrate fully on the other person. This is because true rapport is governed by instinct and is hardwired into our behaviour in a way that cannot be faked for long.

What gets in the way of real listening and rapport?

One of the great pluses of coaching is that it gives the coachee the chance to have that precious commodity – someone else's undivided attention. That is the theory, but in practice a lot can get in the way and this explains why it is rare to feel truly heard or to experience genuine rapport. Here are some of the reasons:

Noise from your internal dialogue. We are all capable of instant judgements about the other person and these are often based on unexamined prejudice. You might think, 'I never did like: men with beards/women under 5 feet tall/ women who wear the hijab/fat men/people with Scottish accents/lawyers' – or whatever the particular preconception is for you.

Believing you already know the answer. This can happen when you are an experienced boss yourself and have seen untold numbers of similar problems to the one brought to you by your coachee. The temptation is to assume that the problem the coachee brings is just like the ones you have met so many times before. This is unlikely to be true, however similar the circumstances may look. Any coach, whether a line-manager coach or a professional executive coach, needs to be especially watchful in the areas where they pride themselves on their expertise. To succeed as a coach, you need the humility to be taught exactly those things that you believe you already know by someone younger or less experienced.

Wanting to reform the coachee. People who enter management often have high ideals. They see themselves as having a duty to put things right, to reform and educate. It can be hard when a team member appears to be taking a wrong path, whether due to personal life issues (e.g. wrecking their health by heavy smoking, drinking too much, staying out for far too many nights a week partying, going on living with an abusive partner) or work-related issues such as displaying timid behaviour at meetings, avoiding promotion or shouting at colleagues. The urge to correct and advise can be overpowering. People who do self-sabotaging behaviour usually know perfectly well that it has adverse consequences but they are ambivalent about change. Telling them what they should do, in their own best interests of course, paradoxically makes it more likely that they will continue to do the unwise behaviour. When you tell them what they should do instead, they will typically reply by defending the behaviour. By giving their reasons out loud for staying as they are, they make it more likely that the status quo will be the outcome. This is based on the compelling evidence that we tend to believe what we hear ourselves say.

Talking about yourself. It can seem like a good idea to say, 'That happened to me, too' because it sounds reassuring, but in doing so you make the assumption that you and the other person are the same – when you are not. What worked for you is unlikely to work for them because in many large and small ways they are totally different from you. Talking about yourself puts the spotlight on you when the whole point of a coaching conversation is that the spotlight is on the coachee, and one of your tasks as a coach is to keep yourself out of the way.

Having pet theories and models that you like to explain. Some people are natural theorists, fascinated by ideas, and the urge to press your latest piece of reading or studying on to your coachee in the spirit of being 'helpful' can seem overwhelming.

Taking notes. This may seem useful, but it interrupts eye contact and the coachee may wonder what you are writing – or may be puzzled about why you sometimes write things down and sometimes don't. It is better to train yourself to listen carefully and to write a brief summary later if you need to.

Psychologizing and interpreting. Knowledge of human nature is valuable, but sometimes a little learning is misleading. Leave speculation about the coachee's relationship with his or her mother, or apparent *neuroses* about work, so-called *lack of self-esteem* or labels such as *narcissistic tendencies* to the psychoanalysts.

Being preoccupied by your own issues. Everyone has problems and sometimes they are intrusive. When there is some distressing event or worry in your own life, it can be even harder than usual to give all your attention to someone else. At its simplest, you will experience this when you have set aside precious time to deal with your inbox, answer your phone calls or write an important paper. You will not want to be interrupted and although you say 'yes, come in', it is not really a good time, so inside you are resentful and only give half your attention to the visitor.

Unawareness. You may have a low level of awareness about how transparent your own behaviour is.

When any of these factors is in play, the other person will be instantly aware of your loss of attention. It only takes a few seconds: snatching a look at your watch, fidgeting, stroking your mobile longingly, glancing at your laptop, looking over the other person's shoulder, sneaking a look at papers, pausing to write notes . . . the inevitable result is that the other person's voice will trail off. It will be impossible for them to go on talking and they will know for certain that you have temporarily lost interest in them.

Inner signs of rapport

Genuine rapport is also known as *congruence* and it comes from being able to switch judgement off. You are curious about the other person. You want to see the world from their perspective. You want to understand them: their ideas, their attitudes, their concerns. You accept that *you do not know them*, nor do you *know what is good for them*. You see only the small part of themselves that they are allowing you to see. When genuine rapport happens, neuroscience has shown that the same areas are active in the brains of the two people concerned (this is known as *mirror neuron activity*). When you are genuinely connected in this way, the body language will look after itself.

Rapport does not mean 'agreeing'

Rapport does not mean that you necessarily agree with the other person. In fact, you may want to disagree profoundly with much of what they are saying – but that comes later. Your effort goes first into understanding them, doing whatever you can to see their world as they see it.

Showing that you are listening

While the physical signs of rapport are useful, you can also give the other person positive proof that you are listening. One of the most constructive ways to do this is through summarizing. Summarizing is a brief encapsulation of what the coachee has said: note that it is actually a summary and not the mindless repetition that seems to be involved in that 'reflecting back' technique that you may have met on some courses. You use the same key words, you are accurate, and you add no interpretation, fanciful speculation or opinion of your own. Knowing that it is your job to summarize can be excellent discipline because you have to concentrate hard. This takes some doing. On courses where we teach this skill, it is comparatively rare for an untrained participant to be able to make a wholly accurate summary of even a five-minute piece of talking from a partner. Most people flounder, either forgetting much of what they have heard or else adding embroiderings of their own – but take heart, practice makes a big difference – and quickly.

Use summarizing whenever the coachee has been talking uninterrupted for a while or when you feel you are getting a bit confused with the ins and outs of their story, when summarizing is a courteous way to interrupt them.

Useful phrases include:

So if I can summarize here . . .

So if I may just interrupt you for a moment, you're saying that . . .

I'm getting a bit lost – can I try a summary?

So let me see if I'm following your train of thought here. In summary, what you think is . . .

Or just a simple

So you feel . . .?

Always end on a question: *Have I got that right?* If you haven't, the coachee can add whatever you have omitted or correct anything you have got wrong. If you have indeed got something wrong, this is no big deal because you have shown willingness to be corrected.

Language matters

Recent research has proved what most of us probably know from experience anyway – that the language we use has a substantial effect on how we think and feel about an issue. This is particularly true of our use of metaphor and simile. In an experiment at Stanford University, Paul Thibodeau and Lera Boroditsky (2011) gave dummy newspapers to the subjects of an experiment. The newspapers contained accounts of crime in a fictional city, including statistics. In one version of the newspaper, the word *beast* was used, describing crime as *preying on* the city. The other version said that crime was a *virus* that was *infecting* the city. These words were used only once. People who read the newspapers were then asked to make suggestions about solving the problem. The group whose newspaper had talked about *beasts* recommended draconian police action – *hunting, hounding, catching, caging, locking up*. The group that had read the newspaper containing the *viral* metaphor recommended social action based on thoughtful diagnosis and cure. These results were only marginally affected by political affiliations. The people in the study were unaware of how the metaphors had influenced their thinking and believed that it was the statistical analysis that had convinced them. There are major implications for coaches here. By listening carefully for the metaphors coachees use, exploring such metaphors and maybe challenging them to find a different one, the coachee may feel quite differently about the problem.

Clean language

This idea comes from the work of the late New Zealand therapist, David Grove, subsequently written up by many others including a good introduction by Wendy Sullivan and Judy Rees (2008). Clean language extends the principles of rapport from body language to words. Grove pointed out how often we use similes and metaphors in our speech, often dozens in the same conversation.

> *I feel as if I'm floating.* You are not literally floating but the word suggests airiness.

> *We have a broken society.* Nothing is physically broken but the metaphor is vivid.

> *I am drowning in work.* Not really drowning but the sensation of being overwhelmed and breathless is there in the metaphor.

> *This presentation is hanging over me like a black cloud. I'm dreading it.* There is no actual black cloud, but the simile suggests threat and worry.

By exploring the other person's language, you demonstrate a willingness to understand their world as they see it. Even more importantly, the coachee develops greater insight into the tangle of feelings that are associated with whatever the problem is.

The phrase 'clean language' means that you notice and then explore the language of the other person and never assume that you know what such language means. You notice any non-verbal signals that the other person is giving – for instance, a frown, a little cough, a tapping foot. Here is an example:

Brandon is giving some informal coaching to Lizzie, a colleague who is annoyed and worried about her relationship with their mutual boss. Lizzie says that the boss treats her discourteously. 'He behaves as if I'm an enemy, a dissident because I have opinions of my own. Are we in Stalinist Russia or McCarthyite America?', she asks indignantly. 'He ignores me in meetings so I end up feeling like I'm some kind of heretic'. When she has meetings with him, she says she feels 'as if I'm getting the Spanish Inquisition treatment and if I don't agree with him, I get the feeling that I'm going to be burned at the stake'.

Instead of ignoring this language, Brandon says, 'So Lizzie, I'm struck by the intensity of your language here, which is all about being, to use your word, a *dissident*. I noticed while you were saying this, you actually drew a throat-cutting sign. [Brandon briefly copies this, smiling as he does so.] You talk about being an enemy, a heretic, McCarthyite, Stalinist Russia, the Inquisition, and being burned at the stake. These are very vivid phrases. Say some more about how this feels to you'.

> Lizzie stops instantly, amazed. 'You've got it in one', she says, that's exactly what it does feel like, persecuted for my opinions and I need to know what to do about it because it can't go on like this!'

The point is that Brandon has immediately created a closer connection with Lizzie simply by commenting neutrally on her language and gesture. By asking her to say more about it, Lizzie deepens her own understanding of the issue. Note that metaphor and simile are invariably emotionally laden and therefore give you reliable clues to what is really going on for that person, since it is feelings rather than thoughts that have the greater power over our behaviour.

Unclean language

David Grove developed a method for exploring clean language, contrasting it with 'unclean' language where the listener assumes they know what the other person wants or means. Here is an example:

> Coachee   I'm at a complete dead end in my career.
> Coach   How could you find a way out?

In this conversation the coach has failed to notice the use of the metaphor *dead end* and has assumed that the coachee wants to find a *way out* – in other words, has substituted a metaphor of their own. It is far too soon in the conversation to ask this question because if the coachee knew the answer, they would not be talking about *dead ends*. Although the coach has had the best of intentions, the effect is that the coachee is subtly demeaned.

The clean language way

A coach who knows about clean language would tackle it in a different way:

Coachee	I'm at a complete dead end in my career.
Coach	Dead end: and what kind of a dead end is that?
Coachee	It's a cul de sac and I've lost my way. I've spent far too long wandering about in this job. Feel lost.
Coach	And . . . lost . . . And that's like . . .?
Coachee	Bewildered. Needing to find some feeling of purpose – of doing something that mattered.
Coach	And if you did have that feeling of purpose, what would that be like?
Coachee	I'd feel fulfilled; I'd be using my strengths.
Coach	So maybe we should look at what those strengths might be?
Coachee	Yes, that would be brilliant.

The full clean language protocol is beyond our brief here, but some questions that we have found useful include:

And what kind of < > is that < >?

And where does that < > come from?

And that's like . . . what?

And what happens next?

And is there anything else about < >?

Tell me more about < >.

What does < > mean for you?

If you had < > what would be happening?

Nominalizations

This ugly word describes abstract words without any specific meaning. Such words are beloved by politicians because they leave the hearer to fill in the blanks for themselves, hence *modernization, improvement, reform.* What kind of *modernization,* exactly? Who would be doing the modernizing and what would they be doing? This is rarely spelt out.

Clarifying abstract words

Where a word has no behaviour attached to it, you are probably in the presence of a nominalization. Don't let these words pass without asking your coachee to explain them, because if you do you will probably be making your own assumptions about what the coachee means, and they may actually mean something quite different. Ask the coachee to explain what the word means for them by spelling out the behaviour that would be visible

> *So when you say you'd like your team to be more **efficient**, what would that mean in terms of what I'd actually see them doing?*

> *You say you are feeling that we're **in a rut** here, but tell me a bit more about how you feel this is showing itself*

Ask for a specific example:

*You said you want me to be more **accessible**, but what specifically do you have in mind?*

Ask for evidence:

*You say we have a **morale problem**, so what's the evidence for that as you see it?*

In the same way, you can press for more specific meaning when people use generalizations such as *always, never* or vague comparisons such as *better, sooner*.

*Do you really mean **always** – or are there some exceptions?*

*If morale was **better**, how much better would that be?*

Here is an example of how it can work in practice:

Howard has come to his boss to complain. He is nineteen and in his first job. Bursting with resentment and a few angry tears already brimming in his eyes, he says, 'I feel so stressed, so incredibly stressed'.

Howard's boss resists the temptation to soothe him by saying, 'Don't worry' (a form of rescuing). Nor does she assume that she knows what *stress* means for Howard because she understands that stress is a nominalization that can mean anything from *got a bit of a headache this morning* to chronic anxiety or frequent panic attacks. She remains calm in the face of his tears.

'So, Howard', she says gently, 'tell me more about the stress. What does this stress mean for you – what's happening?'

'People keep asking me for stuff, pressing me, asking me over and over, and I have to search my files for it, and sometimes they stand over me, and I feel like yelling at them to stop it'.

It turns out that Howard's stress is really just occasional panic about what might happen to him if he is unable to fulfil these requests instantly. The answer is simple: to learn how to say 'yes I can help but not now this minute' to his colleagues, a skill on which his boss is fully able to coach him. She took just a few minutes to inquire into Howard's words, before offering him ten minutes of coaching. Thanks to her skilled questioning, and to the promise of more support when he needed it, Howard found his own solution, so a problem that could have grown to damaging proportions was solved.

Summary

Authentic listening is hard work. However, it is not the mystical process that some management thinkers have suggested. To spare their blushes, we will not actually name the guilty here, but beware if you read something like this:

Profoundly felt, majestician-style deep-hearted listening will attune you to your most inner self and to the essence of the other person's soul, slowing your mind's ear to your mind's eye . . . bla bla . . .

No, honestly it is not that hard. Essentially what it takes is the willingness to suspend the belief that you already know what the other person feels and should do, to make no judgements or assumptions, and to concentrate on truly hearing what they are saying. Use summarizing to check that you understand, keep your own language 'clean', explore interesting metaphors and generalizations. When you do this you will create rapport: the foundation of everything else in coaching.

So if real, deep listening is the first step to effective coaching, what else do you need to have in your tool kit? In the next chapter, we explain how essential it is to know what distinguishes a powerful question from a feeble one and how to provide feedback that will have an impact on performance without destroying morale and trust.

5 CREATING FRESH THINKING: QUESTIONING AND FEEDBACK

Coaching is about raising awareness and increasing the coachee's sense that they can solve their own problems. It is about provoking fresh thinking rather than a droning rehearsal of the same old problem. It is not about giving answers – in other words, telling people what to do – because if this is what happens, no fresh thinking will have occurred. Coaching is at least in part about learning to keep yourself out of the way, so the best coaches are distinguished by the wise questions they ask rather than by the clever answers they give. The first part of this chapter is about how to achieve the seamless, powerful questioning that elevates performance in the coachee. The second part is about how to give and receive feedback, a super-effective and underused tool in getting outstanding results from the people you manage.

Questioning traps

Asking questions seems so easy – surely it is something that anyone can do? But there is all the difference in the world between a question that stimulates and a question that gets an unthinking answer – or between a question that patronizes or induces self-pity and a question that challenges without being aggressive. The secret is acute self-awareness about the nature of the questions you ask and understanding how many traps lie in wait for the unwary coach, not just in how you phrase the questions but in when you ask them.

The most familiar trap for naive questioners is asking closed questions. The give-away is that the answer can be a simple 'yes' or 'no'. You can see this in everyday exchanges:

Q: I was sorry to hear you've been in hospital. Have you recovered okay?

A: Yes thanks

End of conversation. The questioner has signalled that they have little interest in your health because the question is asked in a way that expects the answer 'yes' and therefore closes the topic down. Compare this with someone who conveys that they really would like to know how you are:

> Q: *I was sorry to hear you've been in hospital. How are you doing now?*

> A: *It's taking me a while but the medication helps a lot and I have a great GP. I'm on a rehabilitation scheme that's really good – doing gently increasing amounts of exercise every day.*

So the way you ask the question has a profound impact on the kind of answer you get.

Advice-in-disguise questions

The biggest single trap is asking questions that come from your own agenda but masquerade as being in the coachee's interests.

Robert is Milandra's boss. She has asked for help on designing an induction event for people who have just joined the directorate in which they work. Robert has done well in establishing Milandra's ideal outcome from the conversation. She says she wants to leave the meeting with ideas about how to refresh the opening session, which has typically been run with a dull lecture from one of the directors. Robert is fairly new to the organization and heartily disliked the induction process he experienced himself. He has strong views on the topic, so there is an overwhelming temptation to dominate the conversation by telling Milandra exactly what he would do if he were running the session himself. If he gives in to this temptation, the conversation would soon go like this:

Robert	So have you thought about using an icebreaker?
Milandra	Yes, I have, but I'm not sure what would work with this group.
Robert	Would it be a good idea to use one of those icebreakers where people describe one hope they have about what they want from the event? That's simple isn't it and not as scary as some of those other icebreaker ideas because people will be nervous?
Milandra	Oh, yeah, that would be OK.
Robert	As well as that could you maybe ask them to say what job they were in before?
Milandra	Mmm . . . yes.

Robert wants to be helpful but his three questions begin with a verb: Have you . . . Would it be . . . Could you . . .? *All contain a hidden instruction*. Depending on Milandra's temperament, she will either have to contradict him or, more likely, just meekly agree, so no coaching will have taken place. There are about thirty of these closed constructions in English, including: is/isn't; was/wasn't; have/haven't; could/couldn't; has/hasn't, and so on.

Fortunately, Robert is aware of this danger. To avoid it, he asks these questions:

What are your own ideas about this?

When you've done this kind of event before, what did you choose?

What do you know about the people who will be there?

What's the main problem you think you'll have to solve with this session?

So which of these ideas do you favour?

Once it is clear that Milandra actually has plenty of ideas, Robert tosses in a few of his own, but although she politely acknowledges them, she barely listens – she is already excitedly talking about how she can make this session come alive for the people attending, helping them get over their understandable nervousness and giving them a favourable impression of what it will be like to work in the organization. As she leaves, Robert muses that actually her ideas are better than his own and modestly congratulates himself on having run a successful piece of coaching.

Other questioning traps

Radio and TV interviewers set a bad example here. With a few notable exceptions, they typically ask long, rambling, double or triple questions, perhaps because they believe they are celebrities themselves so it is all about them, not the person they are interviewing. This is fine if they are interviewing politicians, who are trained to blatantly sidestep such babbling and just say what they planned to say anyway regardless of the question. But for an ordinary coachee, the effect is simply bewildering. So if you ask something like the questions below, your coachee will be confused. Which question out of the three are they supposed to answer?

When did this become a problem? And how bad is it for you? Are the others involved as far as you know?

Another variant of this type of question is what can happen when an unaware coach has not clarified what it is they want to ask and launches on a long, thinking-out-loud, I'll-get-there-in-the-end question:

So, you know, I've always been curious about what went on in that department, and I mean, I sort of wondered when it began to be a problem because you looked OK a few weeks ago – you know when we met in the corridor after the meeting, and I'm sorry, oh dear, yes, sorry to hear it's a problem for you but I'm wondering just how bad it really is and whether any of the rest of the team, you know, whether they're feeling the same?

Impact on the coachee: total mystification. What are you being asked, exactly?

The 'why' question

Avoid questions beginning with 'why'. They sound accusatory. A question like *'Why did you do that?'* may evoke memories of being told off by parents or schoolteachers for some repeated petty misdemeanour and the most likely answer will be, just as it was when your coachee was a reproached school child, the stonewalling of 'I don't know'. In any case, enquiring into motivation is rarely productive in coaching. When it is, there are better ways of asking than using a blunt why? These include saying things like:

Talk me through how you got to that opinion . . .

Tell me what your assumptions were . . .

Another problem with the why question is that it encourages futile analysis. Many managers have been trained in analytical questioning. If this has been your own background, you may believe that deep and complex analysis will lead you to one prime cause. Unfortunately, there rarely is one cause of any single problem, but a multiplicity of causes. Focusing on this kind of analysis will have a past rather than a present focus and just clouds the problem further for the coachee. It can have the counter-productive effect of convincing them that it is unsolvable, as happened to Oliver, a manager in the fashion retailing business.

> I had an external coach who prided himself on his *business savvy* as he called it. He constantly asked me why this and why that, pressing me to do what he called *digging deeper* into causes, for instance of the dip in our revenue over the previous year, asking about my approach to customer segmenting, offering me what he called *challenges* to why my own views on this were wrong, asking me for data on competitor chains and why they were doing better than us in the 16–25 market. It was exhausting and I ended up feeling depressed after every session, as doing the analysis and asking *why* never seemed to help with finding out how to move forward.

Collecting endless facts

You are not doing a PhD thesis on your coachee's problem, so there is no need to collect endless factual data: *how much?, when?, how many?, how often?* Keep it simple. The relevant facts will emerge when you ask more powerful questions. Facts are dull much of the time. Asking for more facts is often a way of avoiding the moment when you need to ask more probing and useful questions.

Powerful questions

The only purpose of questions is to open up the coachee's mind. There is no point in going over the same old ground because if you do you will get the same old replies. Coaching questions are powerful when they lead to thoughtful discovery by the coachee.

The best coaching questions are short – somewhere between seven and twelve words. This makes them easy to understand. The shorter they are, the more impact they are likely to have. Good coaching questions are challenging because they cut through excuses or waffle and insist that coachees take responsibility for themselves.

Make it a principle to start every question with the word 'what'. *What* has magical power in coaching. Here's the difference:

Have you already tried to find a solution?

Closed question: can be answered yes or no. In practice, many untrained coaches tag on their own favourite solution, for instance, *Have you tried asking your staff?* This question comes from the coach's agenda. He or she believes that asking the staff is the solution. Thinking done by coachee: nil. In fact, if the coachee has already tried 'asking the staff', their inner response is likely to be annoyance. *Of course I've tried asking the staff – what do you think I am – a complete idiot?*

What have you already tried?

Open question: encourages a longer and probably more honest answer and stops the coach suggesting something the coachee has already thought or done.

Here is another example: *What do you want?* The simplicity of this question belies the profound impact it can have.

Christine is coaching Naomi, a member of her team deeply upset at having failed to get a promotion. At an earlier meeting, Christine had encouraged Naomi to vent some of her feelings of anger and humiliation. Now it is the middle of a much calmer follow-up meeting where they are exploring other career options.

Christine says, 'Naomi, I could see how upset you were and that's very understandable after such a big disappointment, but *what do you want* from your career?'

There is a long pause, always a good sign that the coachee is having to think. Then Naomi says, slowly, 'I want a job where there is more chance to do something useful to society'. There is another long pause and then Naomi blurts out, 'in fact I'd really like to retrain as a teacher'.

Truth has been spoken. The coaching then takes a totally different direction. Christine's role now is to discuss what, if anything, she can do to help make this aspiration a reality.

The other word that is helpful for beginning a question is 'how'. *How* is useful towards the end of the piece of coaching when you are moving to the action phase

How will you do that?

How could you make that happen?

How do you think people will respond?

Sometimes there is no need to ask a question at all – just leave a silence, or say

> *. . . and . . .?*

or

> *Because?*

or

> *Say more about that?*

Closed questions

Closed questions do have their place in a coaching conversation. They are useful when you want to emphasize that it is your role to manage the framework of the conversation or to move it on to the next phase. So these questions expect the answer 'yes'.

Coach question	Coach signal to coachee
Shall we get into it?	The coaching discussion is about to begin in earnest
Is that enough on that topic?	Let's close this phase down
Shall we move on?	
Have we exhausted the options here?	We've probably generated enough ideas so it's time to choose one of them
Shall we stop there?	Time's up!

Styles of question

A coaching session needs to have different types of question for different purposes, so in any one session you may alternate between any or all of these:

Supportive questions where you are encouraging the coachee to tell their story, listening quietly, offering acknowledgement of successes and celebrating learning.

Tell me more . . .

What happened next?

That was a brilliant achievement. What did you learn?

Confronting questions where you may challenge the practicality of some proposed course of action, or point out a discrepancy between what the coachee says they believe in and what they are actually doing. You may need to confront gaps between promises and what is delivered. Confrontation in coaching does not have the aggressive meaning that it can have in everyday usage. It is always done respectfully and calmly

I think you said you'd be able to do x by date y, but that hasn't happened. What got in the way for you?

You seemed very keen for this to happen when we spoke previously, but now you seem much more lukewarm. What's going on for you?

You say you propose going to the warehouse yourself to sort out the supply problem, but how practical is that?

Cathartic questions that encourage the coachee to release some sort of emotion, whether through tears or laughter. Cathartic questions deliberately ask for feelings, not thoughts. While it is easy to express pleasure at someone's joy, it is more challenging to deal with disappointment, fear, anger or sadness. In fact, it may look positively cold not to enquire into feelings, such as when a team member has just received the diagnosis of serious illness or has just experienced some major disappointment such as failing to get the job they wanted. Remember that emotion is the basis of all our decisions and no issue worth attending to in coaching is without an emotional dimension, so it is essential to explore feelings. You might try questions like these:

> *That sounds tough. How are you feeling right now about this?*

> *It must have been disappointing for you. How does it feel when you look back?*

> *What help do you need from me on this?*

> *I'm so sorry to hear your news. How are you coping?*

Many managers who are new to coaching are afraid of strong emotion because they report feeling embarrassed or fearful themselves, such as when the other person is angry or bursts into tears. Some people dread 'causing' tears, but you cannot cause tears – it is a decision to cry, even though the other person may believe that it is not. Crying can be manipulative, whether conscious or not, a tactic to keep the other person at a distance, or it may be a much needed way for the other person to seek the emotional support they need.

Dealing with strong emotion

In our experience, it is impossible to avoid strong emotion in coaching because the more important the issue, the more intense the feelings are likely to be and in practice it is difficult to forecast which part of the conversation may evoke tears – in fact, sometimes tears appear to come out of nothing after an apparently innocuous question. Don't ever try to pretend that tears have not been shed or offer 'there-there' clichés about 'time healing', as such tactics will look as if you are trivializing the other person's pain. See it as a sign that you are on to something too important to brush aside. If a coachee cries or gets angry, it is better to sit quietly, maybe to offer them a tissue if they are crying and just to wait calmly and attentively for the moment to pass. The more quiet empathy you offer, the swifter this is likely to be. You may want to ask, 'What triggered the tears?'

Sometimes, as well as managing all of this, you will have to manage your own responses because something in the coachee's story touches a similar issue for you. The temptation can be to talk about yourself and your own experience, but do this only with the most scrupulous self-questioning by asking yourself, 'Is this about me and my needs, or will it genuinely help the coachee?' Often the answer is that it will not help the coachee at all, in fact it might lure them into trying to coach *you*, which is not the point of the exercise.

Stella is the HR business partner for her department. She has a meeting with Kate, a colleague who has had treatment for breast cancer. Successful surgery and chemotherapy mean that the outlook is good. Kate is only 31 and has discovered that she carries the BRCA2 gene, which predisposes to the disease. Her meeting with Stella is part of a planned Return to Work programme. Stella has her own agenda for the discussion, which is to establish how well Kate is and how she feels about coming back, but thanks to her coaching training she makes no assumptions about what Kate might need from her. Stella is dreading the discussion as she knows it will evoke feelings of sadness about her own mother who has had a long struggle with breast cancer and who also carries the BRCA2 gene, though Stella herself does not.

After some initial greetings, Stella offers the supportive comment, 'This must have been a hugely demanding experience for you'.

Tears immediately appear in Kate's eyes as she says, 'It's been the worst experience of my life. The worst, worst, worst aspect is that I won't be able to have children and my husband is devastated by that and so am I'.

Stella understands that she cannot offer advice or probe this revelation any further, as marital counselling is not her role. Instead, she simply says, 'Yes, I can see that must be devastating' [picking up on the word *devasted* as used by Kate].

Kate's tears now accelerate. It is a struggle for Stella not to join in the tears but she knows that if she does so, she will have lost control of the conversation. So she sits quietly and pats Kate's hand, offering her a tissue, and lets the conversation pause.

'Thank you', says Kate, 'I'll be fine in a moment'. Quickly, the tears stop, Kate sits upright and says, 'I want to get back to work actually, maybe come in part time for a week or so first'.

Privately, Stella is working hard at putting worry about her mother's health out of her mind. So she says, 'When do you think you might do that?'

This turns out to be remarkably easy, as Kate wants to return to part-time work within the next ten days and the discussion ends amicably with agreement about the details.

Stella is pleased that she has been able to use the skills of supportive questioning in coaching without blurting out any 'this happened to my mother' stories, has avoided any danger of meddling in amateur counselling, and has stayed true to her duty to the business.

Providing feedback

You cannot be a line-manager coach without offering feedback – it is one of the most powerful tools at your disposal. The only real duty of a manager is managing performance and the prime way you do this is through feedback. Yet, it is remarkable how rarely feedback is offered and how often it is confused with criticism.

Why we avoid giving or asking for feedback

Self-confidence can be fragile, even in people who seem arrogant. Leaving the apparently inferior status of childhood behind can symbolize never having to hear another judgement on your personality, character or skills in case you hear bad news. We bolster ourselves with the fantasy that we are better than 'most' people (see p. 25), whereas the truth is that the laws of statistics suggest that we are always more likely to be somewhere in the middle. Asking for feedback therefore needs a mature, centred person able to cope with the idea that they may be less than perfect. Hearing feedback that is not totally complimentary takes even more maturity and the willingness to understand that feedback is not an instruction to change – you can choose how much notice you take of it.

It is true that feedback, clumsily given, produces a defensive response. It alerts the amygdala in the brain (p. 75) to danger. So although this is psychological and not physical danger, the brain behaves in just the same way as if the person were under physical attack. In these circumstances feedback will be rejected.

The difference between feedback and criticism

These words are often used synonymously, but in fact they have strikingly different nuances of meaning. When people say they have been given feedback, what they have actually been offered is often criticism. Here are the differences:

Criticism is mostly given when angry and is a way of unloading the giver's anxiety. It is worded in generalities, full of potentially hurtful judgements about the other person's character, has a past-focus and is one-way: giver to receiver, with little chance for the receiver to defend themselves.

Feedback, on the other hand, is given when calm and entirely for the benefit of the receiver as a developmental process. It is specific, factual, and descriptive, avoiding judgements or interpretations about the other person's motivation and character. It is about behaviour not about the person. This greatly increases the chances that it will be heard rather than rejected.

There is also something called *feeble feedback*. This can take many forms:

Vague compliments	*You're rather good at giving presentations*
Vague hints, positive or negative	*Yes, jolly good . . . [voice trails off]* *I thought you might have spent a bit more time on X . . . [frowns, doesn't say how or why]*
Comment is not attributed to anyone in particular, especially not the speaker	***Everyone** feels that this isn't very good* ***People** say you're not a team player*
Non-specific menace	*I think we may need to pull our socks up on X project*

Another version of feeble feedback involves giving a long, convoluted statement in which a minuscule amount of negative criticism is buried. In one organization where this is the default way of handling feedback, it is known among staff as *murder-mystery feedback* because you can never be sure what you have been told but it leaves you with a queasy feeling. This probably arose from older recommendations about providing feedback, known as the 'sandwich technique'. You started with praise, slyly slid the criticism into the middle, and ended with praise. This was supposed to make the criticism acceptable. Actually, what it does is seem purely manipulative. When you are on the receiving end of 'sandwich' feedback, you are listening for the word *but* and don't hear anything else.

> *You are brilliant at getting the audience's attention* **but** *it went pear-shaped in the middle when you showed all those technical slides. Never mind though, you got there in the end because the content was so useful.*

Since most managers understand all of this because they feel just the same about their own performance, a massive collusion takes place. As a boss, you may tell yourself any of the following:

> *It might get better if I just ignore it.*

> *If I give them praise, they might think I don't mean it or it might seem patronizing.*

> *Who am I to tell this person what my opinion is?*

> *I might be wrong.*

> *I might upset or hurt him/her and I couldn't cope with that.*

> *They might hate me and I want them to like me.*

> *I'll tackle it next week.*

> *I'll ask my boss to do it instead.*

Team members don't want to hear feedback and managers don't want to give it, so feedback is rare, but as a coach you cannot afford to let this happen. Coaching is about raising self-awareness and feedback is one of the prime ways to do it. One way to think about this is captured in a well-known tool, now more than fifty years old but none the worse for that, called the Johari Window (see Figure 5.1). The exotic-sounding name is merely a combination of the names of its two inventors, Joe Luft and Harry Ingram.

The size of the four 'windows' will vary, depending on how and what feedback you ask for and how open you are to taking notice of it when you are given it. So, for instance, your blind area might be massive compared with the other 'windows': others see you and your behaviour clearly but you do not see these things yourself. When this is the case, the handicaps are enormous and ultimately can result in career derailment. Asking for and receiving feedback

	Known by Self	Unknown by Self
Known by Others	Open Area: what I know and what others know	Blind Area: known to others but not to me
Unknown by Others	Hidden Area: what I know but others don't	Unknown Area: unknown to everyone including me

Figure 5.1 The Johari Window

increases the size of the open area and potentially reduces the sizes of the hidden, blind and unknown areas. The open area can be developed through self-disclosure, which reduces the hidden area.

The unknown area can be reduced in different ways: by observation from others, including coaching feedback; by self-discovery through coaching questions, or by mutual enlightenment.

The objective of coaching and of giving feedback is to increase the size of the open window, thus raising awareness and helping the coachee to choose to behave differently in the future.

The essence of genuine feedback is that it separates fact from opinion. Most of what passes for feedback is entirely opinion and couched in unhelpful generalities. Here are some examples:

- *You took far too long on that task.* Comment: How long is *too long*, exactly? What was too long?
- *You were brilliant at that meeting.* Comment: Nice to hear, but what, specifically, was brilliant?
- *You're very unpunctual.* Comment: An attack on the person's character rather than their behaviour and a generality. Unpunctual all the time? Where's the evidence? Five minutes late or several hours?
- You're very good at analysing things. Comment: Clearly a compliment, but what does 'good' mean, and analysing what 'things'? And what it is it about 'analysing' that is so important?

As chances to raise self-awareness and influence future behaviour, these statements are hopelessly inadequate.

Six easy steps to giving feedback that will be heard

If you follow this protocol, you will find that feedback becomes easy to give and easy for the other person to hear and accept.

Step 1. Get over your reluctance to do it: it's in the coachee's interests and they will be taking responsibility for how they receive it. It's up to them how they react.

Step 2. Ask permission: 'May I offer you some feedback?' Note that no one ever refuses, even though they may say 'yes' apprehensively.

Step 3. Describe what you have observed, using phrases like: *What I noticed . . ., I observed . . ., I heard . . ., I saw . . .* And stick to the facts. Don't interpret. So don't say, 'You were bored and disengaged in that meeting', because you will have no idea whether or not this is true – you do not have the X-ray vision to reveal the other person's motivation, so saying 'you were bored' is an interpretation – an opinion. Do say what you actually saw: 'I noticed you were doodling on your pad for the first ten minutes of the meeting and didn't look up at all'.

Step 4. Describe the impact on you. This means you own your opinion and allow the hearer to separate the facts (what you saw or heard) from your opinion (how this landed with you). Other advantages are that it is impossible for the other person to argue with how you experienced their behaviour, especially since you are not claiming that the impact on you was necessarily the same as it might have been for others.

I noticed you were doodling on your pad for the first ten minutes of the meeting and didn't look up at all. So the impact on me was that I didn't know if you were going to

speak at all and I was distracted by the noise of your pen and I kept wondering what you were drawing.

Step 5. Ask for the coachee's response. Use phrases like:

So I'm wondering: what was going on for you?

What links do you see between this and feedback other people have given you?

How did it seem to you?

What do you think?

Step 6. Agree how you will work on whatever comes out of this discussion.

Feedback in practice

Feedback is often discussed as if it is invariably about a problem, but it works just as effectively and perhaps more so when what you want to emphasize is how well someone has done. When you do this, you increase the chances of reinforcing the desirable behaviour. So this is the pleasant part of providing feedback: offering someone closely made observation of good performance.

> Olivia is coaching Fraser, a new member of her team. Fraser is personable and clever. Privately, although Olivia is more senior in theory, she will admit to being a little in awe of Fraser, so has to struggle to offer him feedback, quelling that internal voice that says, 'who am I to offer this clever guy feedback?'
>
> Olivia has accompanied Fraser at a successful meeting to negotiate a contract with a customer, having agreed in a mini-coaching session ahead of the meeting to

letting him take the lead role. She follows all the other feedback steps, first of all asking permission and seeing that Fraser nods immediately. She sticks scrupulously to the feedback protocol, describing everything she saw, for instance: 'I noticed that in the first ten minutes you did very little talking, you just drew him out with respectful questions [he describes some of them]. So you knew exactly what his needs were. Then you asked if it would be okay to put forward what we needed. That was the turning point'.

Olivia then describes the impact on her: 'I felt immediate relief: I could see that we were going to get what we needed and I thought you handled it very skilfully'.

Olivia now asks Fraser what he made of it. Fraser says: 'I was aware that I was a bit tense at the beginning, but I was pleased to be able to get on with it just with your silent support and I knew I could bring you in if I had to. Yes, I felt it went well, but I'd appreciate your ideas on how we follow that up'.

The session now turns to how to make the follow-up process successful.

Results of this session: Olivia has reinforced an already good relationship, has increased her own confidence as a boss and has sent a clear message to Fraser about the behaviour she admires and wants to see continue.

Relaying a more negative message

This is harder, but the same principles apply. Typically you will be offering feedback on behaviour that is in the other person's blind spot (see above): something that everyone around them sees clearly but they do not. The normal reason for this is that when guilty of behaviour that is unhelpful, hurtful or damaging to others, we fail to distinguish between intention and impact. We judge ourselves by our good intentions but others cannot see our intentions, they judge by our behaviour and that behaviour may give a very different impression. Here are some examples:

> Zena is a highly motivated and hard-working manager in retail banking. She sees herself as firm but fair, dedicated to achieving high standards and expects others to understand that driving up performance in everyone's interests is what motivates her. However, what her direct reports see is her abrasive manner and clipped instructions. They are afraid of her and avoid her whenever they can.

> Jonathan regards himself as 'the truth-teller' as one of a team of in-house legal advisors. He is intelligent, lively – and at his best – witty. He believes it takes courage to speak up and to voice criticisms which challenge the status quo and which are in the best interests of the group. He does not understand that his comments can come across as sarcastic, negative, and personally hurtful – and that his colleagues believe he is becoming an annoying show off.

Intention and impact: the difference

The first task of a boss if you are coaching someone like Zena or Jonathan is to raise their levels of awareness about the gap between intention and impact. When Jonathan's boss does this, he wants to keep Jonathan in his team because he is an able lawyer, but is aware that this behaviour could be damaging to the team if it persists and career limiting for Jonathan. He chooses to raise the issue immediately after a team meeting where Jonathan's behaviour has been particularly extreme. Having asked to see him and then asked permission to offer feedback, he says:

'I wanted to talk to you today, Jon, because I was perturbed by some of your comments. When you said to Peter that you thought he was "camp as a row of tents" and to Alison that she "gave toadying a bad name", I wondered what your intention was'. Jonathan's boss shows no sign of his disapproval at this stage, even though in fact he does strongly disapprove. He is merely asking about intention.

Jonathan says readily, 'Just a bit of fun – intended to wake people up a bit and stop the sycophancy I see them doing around you'.

'I see', says the boss, 'so it was a positive intention. But the impact on me was pure embarrassment and I noticed that Peter looked upset and Alison blushed. It certainly landed very badly with me'.

Jonathan's boss then explores similar incidents and asks him for responses. 'I didn't mean any harm – they shouldn't take it so personally', Jonathan replies, looking annoyed and sulky.

'But actually they did take it personally. And I have too when you've said similar things to me [he gives some examples]'. The conversation then turns to what Jonathan might do to make amends. Now much more

---

humble, Jonathan offers to make immediate apologies to the two colleagues and he and his boss agree to meet again to discuss how he might rein in this behaviour in future.

Nightmare scenario

When we ask people on our training courses about difficult situations in which they have had to give feedback, there is almost always someone in the group who confesses to having avoided offering a colleague feedback on personal appearance or hygiene. But actually the same principles will work, even in cases where mutual embarrassment seems assured. If people have problems of this sort, their prospects for promotion – and sometimes even for keeping their jobs – are likely to be severely limited. Everyone else is acutely aware of the problem but the person themselves appears not to be. Here is a manager in a housing association, describing how he used feedback to deal with this issue:

It helped that I was new. In my first week as part of my 'listening exercise' everyone mentioned, though in hushed voices, that there was 'a problem with Gemma'. Putting it bluntly, she smelled awful. No one had confronted her. She had, inexplicably, been recently promoted so that she was dealing directly with members of the public in our 'One-Stop Shop' for tenants. At least one tenant had complained but nothing had been done. Colleagues had done lots of hinting, such as talking about 'showers', 'baths', and 'washing machines' in her presence. One person had done a lot of aggressive sniffing, complaining that 'there's a funny smell round here' but no one had directly offered her feedback. As soon as I met her I realized they were right. In fact, any room she'd been in still smelled afterwards. It was not acceptable. I knew there was no point in doing that 'sandwich technique' and that I had to come straight out with it. I arranged to meet her in my office and said immediately she had sat down, 'Gemma, this is not going to be easy to say, but I need to give you some feedback. Are you up for that?' She looked startled and squirmed around in her seat but said, 'Yes, 's'pose so' in a grumpy way.

I said, 'The problem is that you have a strong body odour and it's not pleasant. I'm not just going on what other people have told me here, though many others have in fact mentioned it to me and I gather there has been a complaint from a tenant at the One-Stop Shop, but I have noticed it myself, in fact I'm very aware of it now. It seems like a combination of sweat and clothes that haven't been washed very often. And when I shared the lift with you yesterday, it was really overpowering'.

She began to cry at this point, but I had the tissues ready. I pressed on, saying, 'The impact on me is that I feel really embarrassed having to raise it with you but I feel it's my duty as your boss to discuss it, as it just is not acceptable when you share an office with so many other people and work directly with the public'.

Then I stopped and, aware that I needed to ask for her reactions, said, 'So how do you feel about this?'

Then out poured a lot of stuff about having to share a small flat with her younger brothers, no money for clothes, no washing machine, didn't know about the smell, life in confusion after the breakdown of a relationship and death of both parents, all in the same year.

I summarized all of this using a lot of quiet empathy, and then said, 'So what's the solution?'

In a nutshell, it was: find a buddy in the department, deep laundering for all her clothes at the local launderette, twice if necessary, new hygiene regime; promise of my support to combat 'humiliation' (*Does everyone know about this? Well, yes they do . . .*). I made it clear it could not continue and we agreed to meet at the end of the week. This story does not have a happy ending. She went off sick a few days later and after intervention from Occupational Health, left soon after that. Their view was that her real problem was self-neglect for all the reasons she'd hinted at. However, I feel pleased that I was able to tackle her in a way that was respectful and in coaching style. I accepted that it was her choice whether or not to change but that I had to make it clear to her that it was not an option to continue as she was.

Feedback in the here and now

You have a great opportunity in every coaching session to use instant feedback. Rather than assuming that you are somehow immune to any effect the team member is having on you and politely suppressing it, you notice it and offer it. The feedback cannot be denied because it has happened right there. Here are some examples:

Team member behaviour	Manager-coach says . . .
Suddenly looks tired in the session	I notice you've been slumped down in your chair for the last five minutes, whereas before that you were looking animated. What's going on for you?
Denies responsibility for upsetting and intimidating colleagues and while doing so, shouts at boss	So I can see that you don't like this idea but I notice that when you were denying you'd upset them, you raised your voice like this [*copies it*] and I'm wondering whether this is what people mean by saying you can be 'intimidating'. I felt quite frightened myself when you did that. What do you think?
Issue is that she has problems with assertiveness. Exasperates colleagues by constant and unnecessary apologizing. Uses the word *sorry* many times in the actual coaching session	While we've been talking, I've noticed that you've used the word 'sorry' six times [*briefly runs through them*]. Once I'd noticed this I began to get a bit annoyed by it and I'm thinking that this might be the same as the impact it has on other people.
Coachee then apologizes for apologizing	OK – you're doing it now!
	[*both laugh*]

Asking for feedback on yourself

It is every bit as difficult to ask for feedback as it is to give it, and for the same reasons. But a self-aware manager knows that in every relationship there are two sides and that often we are part of the problem as well as part of the solution. It is easy to ignore the hints that people may not like some aspect of your behaviour or to assume that where they disapprove they are deluded or too junior to matter. You see this most notably when political or celebrity careers crash spectacularly. The reasons are virtually always that the person concerned has swallowed their own myths and believes that the rules do not apply to them, so they can pursue adulterous affairs, behave corruptly, assume that rules are for unimportant 'little' people, not for them, or bully and manipulate as they like. In retrospect, there have always been people who have warned them, but they have paid no attention. There are many examples from the world of politics where senior politicians in office can quickly become seduced by a sense of their own importance, even though they must know rationally that most ministerial careers are brief.

Part of the deal as a manager-coach is that you are brave enough to ask for feedback on yourself. There is strong evidence that high self-awareness on the part of a boss correlate with impressive bottom-line performance. In several studies, chief executives who had a realistic view of themselves, and whose self-report agreed closely with how others saw them, were likely to be achieving a superior bottom-line performance where their organizations were concerned. Remember that what you hear may be criticism, may be clumsily offered, and may just be one person's warped opinion – or it may be a valuable clue to what many others think and feel about you. It is your choice how you respond. Feedback is just that: it is not an instruction to change.

Excuses

Most of us have a whole armoury of excuses about why we don't ask for feedback. None stands up to scrutiny.

Excuse	More honest explanation
They are ignorant. They don't understand the intense pressures I am under	They just see and respond to your behaviour, but if you can find a calm way of explaining the pressures, that might help
I already know this	If so why aren't you paying attention? You may know the headlines but do you know for sure how strongly (or not) people feel about it?
Different people see me in different ways, so what's the point?	It's not about consistency. It is usually productive to see which groups of people you impress and which are less impressed
I might hear something I don't like	True, but it's up to you how you respond. And you may hear lots of affirming things that you will like
I am my own harshest critic, so I don't need to know what other people think	Maybe, but other people may have different opinions and their views might be influential
How would I cope if I hear stuff I don't like?	Yes, this is the core fear, but you would cope – at the very least you could just dismiss the whole thing – or even learn from it. People hold these views of you whether you know such views or not, so you might as well know what they are

Asking for feedback is a little like reverse engineering, starting with an apparently finished article (a vague statement in this case) and systematically investigating its component parts. You are using the same techniques as when you give feedback, but you may have to be skilful and persistent in how you ask.

Steps to asking for feedback

Step 1: Get over your reluctance. You will be modelling openness, courage, and humility, all desirable qualities in a manager.

Step 2: Ask your opening question. This will depend on the circumstances, but start by asking permission: 'May I ask you for some feedback?' The other person may look a little startled or uncomfortable, but no one ever says no.

You then ask how your style strikes the other person, what they observe about how you manage them, what they like and like less. Alternatively, you might ask how the other person feels you have contributed to whatever the issue is that you are discussing.

Step 3: The chances are that you will get timid and generalized responses, e.g. 'It's great', 'You're better than that last boss', 'Fine'.

Step 4: Press for specifics. 'When you say I am "quite consultative", could you give me a specific example?' Note that you are looking for behaviourally based evidence.

Step 5: If you hear something negative, explore it. Don't do what the majority of people do in such circumstances, which is to rush to defend yourself. Instead, ask again for evidence: 'Tell me more about that', or 'What was the impact on you?'

Step 6: Give your response.

Step 7: Thank the other person. Truly, they have bestowed a rare gift on you.

Paula is having a challenging coaching conversation with Astrid, one of her buying team in a retail organization. Astrid's performance has been mediocre, she likes to work solo when ideally she should be working as part of a close-knit team and merchandising colleagues have been critical. Sales are down 20 per cent on last year. Paula has given Astrid some tough feedback and Astrid's face is suddenly suffused with redness. She bursts out: 'None of this is down to me, it's all about the global economy and none of our competitors has reported good results, and I would have been able to do so much better if you weren't so inaccessible!'

Paula stifles her annoyance at Astrid's refusal to accept responsibility for her poor results. She knows that the point about competitors has some truth but it is not the whole story. She believes she is as accessible as any busy senior manager can be and it is maddening to hear this criticism stated so rudely. However, she stays calm, recognizes that there might just be some useful feedback here, and that the point about 'inaccessibility' is a generalization and says, 'Inaccessible? Can you give me an example of when I have been inaccessible?'

Astrid reels off a list of times when Paula has been on foreign trips or otherwise away from her office. Paula summarizes, 'So you feel my frequent absences have made it more difficult for you?' Being listened to so attentively has calmed Astrid down and she apologizes for shouting. There is then a productive discussion about how far phone calls, video conferencing, emails, Skype, and texts are an acceptable substitute for a face-to-face discussion. Paula sees that although she rejects the generalization, her systems for arranging contact with her team have been less than perfect and she resolves to change them.

Whether or not coaching can change Astrid's behaviour is a bigger question. When people are so firmly fixed in the 'I am a victim' position, the chances are that it will not.

Summary

Asking powerful questions, offering and soliciting feedback are essential skills for a manager-coach. Both these techniques are ways of servicing the main aims of coaching, which are to raise self-awareness and to make mindful choices. Good questioning means avoiding everyday traps such as asking questions that come from your own agenda or making the question too long to be easily understood. Good coaching questions are short and will usually begin 'What . . .?' The skilled manager-coach must tackle any personal squeamishness about offering and asking for feedback and be careful to understand the differences between feedback and criticism. Skilfully given, feedback breaks through our blind spots, especially if it is offered on the basis of behaviour that the coachee actually does during the coaching session itself, an approach known as 'feedback in the here and now'. Asking for feedback is equally powerful and for the same reasons.

There is an art in asking questions in the right order and managing the whole process, which is where OSCAR comes in, the focus of the next chapter.

MANAGING THE COACHING CONVERSATION: OSCAR

A coaching session is not just a nice chat. It is purposeful and needs to be carefully managed. But how? In our early days of training line managers as coaches, we realized how often a potentially excellent coach would ask a good question but at the wrong point in the discussion. For instance, they would do something like this:

Coach	So what do you want to get out of this conversation?
Coachee	I need to solve the problem of how to get better performance out of X (team member).
Coach	Okay – so what are the options?
Coachee	Err . . .

The coach's first question is fine because it establishes the goal, and the second question is also a good question, but it needs to be asked much later in the conversation. If the coachee had already been fully aware of what the options were, he or she would probably not need to ask for the coaching.

People sometimes struggle to distinguish between the coachee's job – finding their own solutions – and the coach's job, which is to provide the 'process framework' of the conversation. It is always the coach's job to manage how the discussion runs, for instance knowing how to open it, managing the time and pace, deciding which phase of the conversation you are in and moving from one phase to another, ending neatly. In this chapter, we introduce you to the OSCAR model as an easy and effective way to do all of this. Bearing the mnemonic of OSCAR in mind will help you understand where you are in the conversation and keep you on track to get to a point where something significant changes for the coachee.

There are many coaching models with slick acronyms to help you remember them. Karen Whittleworth and Andrew Gilbert, co-authors of this book, developed the OSCAR model as a way of providing practical help on all of this. OSCAR stands for Outcome, Situation, Choices and Consequences, Action, and Review. It builds on the well-known GROW model (Goal, Reality, Options, What next). GROW has been very useful as a simple way of remembering the framework of a coaching conversation and has proved its value over many years, but we believe OSCAR is more effective for managers. The Goal part of GROW is similar to the Outcome stage of OSCAR. Reality in GROW resembles Situation, and Options is similar to Choices and Consequences. OSCAR is more closely related to managerial contexts because the Situation phase explicitly involves a 'gap analysis', and the Choices and Consequences phase gives far more scope for weighing up risks. Similarly, the Action and Review phases of OSCAR allow for more specific emphasis on what exactly the coachee is going to do and how they will be held to account, a vital part of any manager's responsibility.

OUTCOME The destination	• What would you like to achieve from today's session? (short-term outcome?) • What is your long-term outcome? • What would long-term success look like? What would be different? This is where you help the coachee clarify the outcome they want around the issue they have raised.
SITUATION The starting point	• What is the current situation? • What's actually happening? • Who is involved? • What makes it an issue now? This is where you get clarity around where the coachee is right now. The purpose is to raise the awareness of the person being coached and the questioning in this section is for the benefit of the person being coached not the coach.

CHOICES and CONSEQUENCES The route options	• What have you already tried? • What choices do you have? • What options can you choose from? • What are the consequences of each choice? • Which choices have the best consequences? This is where you help the coachee to generate as many alternative courses of actions as possible, increasing their awareness about the consequences (upsides and downsides) of each choice.
ACTIONS The detailed plan	• What actions will you take? • What will you do next? • How will you do it? • When will you do it, with whom? • On a scale of 1 to 10, how willing are you to take those actions? This is where you help the coachee review the options generated, to clarify the steps forward, and to take responsibility for their own action plan.
REVIEW Making sure you are on track	• What steps will you take to review your progress? • When are we going to get together to review progress? • What actions are you actually taking? • How far are the actions moving you towards your outcome? This is where you help the coachee to check that they are on course. This helps you as their boss to be fully informed about what your team member is doing and why.

The OSCAR model provides you with a simple structure that helps to keep the coaching process focused, structured, and time-effective.

Here is how it works at each stage in a little more detail.

Outcome

The effect of having clear outcomes and goals has been studied extensively, such as in sport, where not just reputation but also big money can be at stake, depending on how an athlete performs. This research, and much other research into motivation at work, shows that when you are clear what your goal is, your attention is focused, and the chances are increased that your behaviour will change. A goal you set yourself is far more motivating than one set by someone else. A goal with some stretch and challenge is more motivating than one that seems too easy, and a goal that works in stages is more likely to be met than some overarching goal that appears daunting. Any goal needs to be a snug fit with your personal values, so it would be a waste of time, for instance, to suggest a goal like 'Appoint 20 per cent more women' to someone who felt strongly that such quotas were intrinsically unfair and unworkable.

Altogether, people with well-formed outcomes achieve much more than those who do not. Successful coaching sessions typically involve working with the coachee to develop a deeper understanding of the outcome they want. Clarifying the short-term outcome helps the coachee to focus on what they want from the immediate coaching conversation, while clarifying the longer-term outcome helps the coachee to become clear about what they want in the more distant future. Most people tend to think in terms of problems rather than outcomes. Getting your coachee to think in terms of outcomes helps them to focus on solutions rather than excuses.

When you do not have a clear outcome agreed for a coaching conversation, the effects are immediate and they are all undesirable. The conversation begins to ramble, the coachee starts to offer a mass of detail, the coach begins to worry about whether they are being helpful, loses the thread or tries to analyse the issues and ends up offering advice and solutions, so although the conversation might appear to be 'helpful' and the coachee politely thanks you, coaching it has not been.

A clearly defined outcome is one of the best ways to ensure that the coaching conversation goes well, but it can be more challenging than it looks to do this well because coachees do not necessarily arrive with a neatly phrased outcome; in fact, they are far more likely to present with one that is fuzzy and imperfectly formed.

Here are some of the typical ways a coachee can present an issue:

Coachee says	Why you can't work on it as presented
I want to be more confident	It's far too big. Lack of confidence is a life position reinforced by years of habit and you are not going to 'cure' it in a single conversation, though you might be able to work helpfully on one aspect, such as giving the opening five minutes of a presentation more confidently
I can't stand X (a colleague) – he's noisy and in our open plan office he's getting on my nerves	You haven't got X in the room. The coachee has come to complain and pass the problem on to you. Coaching only works on the bit of the problem that the coachee owns: in this case, his own responsibility for dealing with X
I need help with my time management	'Time management' is just a label and far too vague to work on. What aspect of it exactly does the coachee want to concentrate on?

Continued

Coachee says	Why you can't work on it as presented
I must get myself up to speed on project management	The word 'I must' is the give-away. Who says? Where is the personal ownership?
HR says I could do with some coaching on how I deal with people	Whoa! First of all, this is HR's idea not the coachee's and 'dealing with people' is a subject that is both enormous and vague
I can't get myself motivated to organize the office move	You can't work on a negative – how not to do something or avoid something, only on a positive – how *to do* something

We find that the term 'outcome' is much more powerful and acceptable than the word 'goal', which often is linked with targets that are imposed by someone else. So a goal like 'How do I take out 10 per cent of costs?' is clear, but it is an externally and organizationally imposed goal that, as it stands, has no discernible connection with the individual's own need and will therefore have low power to motivate. The words *goal* and *target* are often associated with a feeling of demand and pressure. By contrast, the word *outcome* is often anchored to a feeling of collaboration and involvement. Positive outcomes are often achieved in an environment of partnership and mutual support – they are intrinsic motivators. Telling someone to achieve a target is very different from allowing an outcome to be defined as an alliance and developing a mutually agreed action plan to achieve it.

It is vital to be aware of the difference between an overall aim, such as 'getting clarity about my next career move', and the outcome from any specific conversation. In this example, Steve neatly distinguishes between these two types of outcome when he is coaching Gwyneth.

Gwyneth has just had her fiftieth birthday and is feeling frustrated with her job as team leader in a social services department. She has already had one useful conversation with her boss Steve about her feelings of restlessness and her boredom with high levels of admin. She had briefly mentioned the notion of returning to the Child Protection team, work she had enjoyed a lot in her earlier career. She has come back for a second discussion. After welcoming her, Steve asks her a good outcome-defining question: 'So Gwyneth, what's our focus for this conversation?'

Gwyneth is an eager talker and avoids answering directly, repeating in rapid-fire sentences much of what she had said in the first conversation about needing to refocus her career and her impatience with her current role.

Steve says, 'Yes, I understand that your overall aim is to reconsider your career, but what do you need from me in this conversation today? We've got about twenty minutes before I set off for my meeting'.

There is a short pause. Gwyneth says, this time a lot more slowly, 'I'd like to look at the pros and cons of going back to fieldwork with Child Protection'.

The words *in this conversation* and the tactful reminder that time is limited are crucial. They force Gwyneth to narrow down to a specific outcome. Just to reinforce that this is indeed what they are going to do, Steve says: 'So it would be a good outcome for you if you left here today with more clarity about whether going back to fieldwork would be a good choice?'

'Yes', says Gwyneth – and the coaching conversation can now take off.

This example is a reminder that getting clarity about an issue is a perfectly acceptable outcome from a coaching conversation. In fact, a coachee rarely wants to make an important life decision such as a change of career in the coaching discussion itself. 'Get clearer about X or Y issue' is usually enough.

Other useful outcome-setting questions

Here are some more questions that may help in this phase of the coaching:

> *So if you left here today with what you wanted, what would have changed for you?*

> *What help do you need from me in relation to [whatever the issue is]?*

> *What's the outcome you need from this conversation?*

Trigger words from the coachee showing you that you do indeed have an outcome you can work on are:

> *I'd like to know how to . . .* This is because the words *how to* are usually followed by some behavioural description.

> *I'd like to get clearer about . . .* This phrase will usually introduce a dilemma that is puzzling the coachee.

Situation

This phase of the conversation is really a 'gap analysis' – a familiar concept from management consultancy. Given that you have established the ideal solution, where are you now? What's the gap between the ideal and the present? The temptation here is to spend far too long on dull facts. Once the central facts have been established, there is usually little point in digging for yet more detail. In our experience, many line-manager coaches are at risk of spending too much time focusing on the current situation, thus getting over-involved in the problem rather than focusing on the outcome. If this is a danger for you, it will most probably be because you have been trained in an investigative enquiry technique where the presumption is that you are acting like some kind of managerial detective and that if you ask for enough data, the bedrock cause will eventually reveal itself. This is a false trail in coaching. Instead, the emphasis should be on the size of the gap and on the psychological and actual cost of staying stuck. The purpose of this phase of the coaching is to understand the implications of the current situation and to increase energy for change rather than trying to find the solution. It is too soon to find the solution because you know nothing about the thinking the coachee has already done and even less about what is keeping them stuck. Here is an example.

Laura is Harry's boss and has asked him to give a presentation at a conference for suppliers. She could have fulfilled this engagement herself but has decided instead to take some holiday leave. Harry has accepted but she knows he is nervous. She's asked him to drop into her office to discuss his progress. After the usual greetings, Laura asks Harry how he is feeling about the presentation. Harry replies, looking a little shifty, that he has done very little because he's been 'too busy' and begins to describe in detail how busy he has been.

Laura politely but firmly cuts in because she is aware that Harry's alleged busyness is probably a smokescreen and in any case it is irrelevant to the topic, so she says, 'I asked you to pop in today because I suspected as much and I want to help you as much as I can. We've got ten minutes today. What do you need from me in this conversation to get you back on track?'

Harry mumbles a bit and after a little more probing, says that he doesn't know how to structure his talk. Laura reframes this into a workable outcome: 'So it would be useful to discuss how to create the structure for your talk?' It will probably be wise for Laura to repeat the Outcome, just to focus her own and Harry's attention on what it is they want to achieve. So she says, 'Just to be clear, Harry, our aim is how to create a structure for your presentation'. Harry agrees.

So now Laura is at S for Situation and needs to contrast the desirable outcome with where Harry is currently. 'Tell me how far you've got now', she asks. Harry briefly outlines some notably sketchy ideas while Laura listens quietly, privately thinking how quickly she could have written the presentation herself, reining in her impatience and reminding herself that the conference will be a developmental experience for Harry, and that she needs to ensure that he does a reasonable job because her own reputation will be on the line as well as his. She says, 'So there are five working days between now and having to submit your slides. How much time do you think you will need to devote to it?' The answer is 'at least a day'.

Laura now sets out to establish the implications of ignoring the gap between the current situation and the ideal. 'What happens if you don't set aside that time?', she asks.

Harry looks thoroughly alarmed. 'You will be mightily displeased with me and I'll fall flat on my face because I'll be scrabbling it together at the last minute', he says.

'Exactly', says Laura, smiling. 'What's preventing you getting on with it?'

Harry slowly and sheepishly confesses to paralysing fear. So now his real need has been exposed. The gap has been established and the consequences of more delay clearly set out and the causes of the delay (fear) named. Laura can now continue with the conversation by moving to the two C's: Choices and Consequences.

Useful questions to establish the current situation include:

What's the current state of affairs?

What's at stake for you (business, family, health, colleagues, money – as appropriate)?

What's the gap between what you want (the ideal outcome) and the current state?

What's standing in the way?

What's your own responsibility here?

What will happen if you do nothing?

How important is this issue on a scale of 1–10?

How much energy, also on a scale of 1–10, do you have to tackle it?

Blind spots

With some coaches, you will be dealing with blind spots (p. 127). You and others know there is a problem but the coachee does not recognize it. This is where the skills of feedback (p. 124) are vital and the Situation phase of the

OSCAR model is the place to use it. For more on this, see 'Coaching an unaware coachee' (p. 182).

Choices and Consequences

The essence of coaching is increasing people's sense of resourcefulness. When you feel resourceful you feel in control, and when you feel in control you feel confident. That vital feeling of control comes from knowing that there are choices you can make. By using OSCAR, the coach/manager encourages the team member to generate a number of options to choose from. This is not always as easy as it looks.

Coachee says	Implication/private dialogue inside coachee's head
I haven't got a choice. I must do x or y	I am helpless; I need rescuing
I don't know – what do you think?	I'm afraid of speaking up – you, O Mighty Boss, know best so why don't you just tell me and save us the trouble of having this conversation?
It's down to someone else to do this	Afraid of taking responsibility or genuine confusion about roles
It's all out of my control	Unwilling to look at which bit *is* within their control

When any of us says something like this, we are stuck in an unaware place – unaware, that is, that going on doing what we have always done (the default position) is in itself a choice. In practice, there are always at least two possible choices: doing nothing and doing something. Doing nothing can be the most popular choice, so asking what the consequences are of doing nothing is often the first step to raising energy for doing something different.

Brainstorming

This is a useful way of generating options and the benefit of it is that you can join in – as long as you stick to some simple rules. These are that you ask permission to do some brainstorming – labelling it like this shows the coachee that you are going to do something different. You then explain the rules. These are:

- You each spark each other off to list as many ideas as you can on a piece of paper. Write everything down, however silly or irrelevant it seems. There should be a playful, creative, light feel to the conversation.
- The ideas should deliberately include those that are obviously daft, as this stimulates further creative thinking, including generating ideas that are sensible.
- No evaluation whatsoever is allowed at this point – no sighs, no self-editing (*Oh, that's a stupid idea*) or raised eyebrows.
- When you have exhausted the ideas, you ask the coachee to tick or highlight any that seem interesting enough to explore further. Note that it is important for the coachee to do this – not you, as you are encouraging their thinking rather than your own.
- You then say: 'How will you evaluate these ideas?' You are asking for their criteria, which are usually about practicality, cost, time, and fit with personal values.

Remember that although you join in the generation of ideas, it is the coachee who makes the choices and names the criteria. This should produce at least three workable ideas.

Here is how Nancy uses the technique with Maya.

Maya manages the front of house waiting team in the hotel where she works and Nancy is her boss. There have been complaints from guests about the quality of the breakfast service. Nancy has established the outcome for the conversation, which is to come up with a workable plan for improvement. Maya seems a bit stuck and has done a little shoulder-shrugging, suggesting that the real problem is with the kitchen and with the management ban on increasing the numbers of waiting staff, not with her team.

'Let's do a brainstorm', says Nancy and explains the 'rules'. Together they come up with about a dozen ideas, including: investing in self-serve coffee machines, doing away with unhelpful job demarcations between roles, Maya herself taking part in the actual service, having a quicker way of making coffee, directing the waiting team more consciously or re-training them, replenishing the hot food more frequently, having a daily meeting with the breakfast chef to anticipate demand based on room occupancy, staggering the times the waiting staff come on shift, and so on.

Then Nancy says, 'So what are your criteria here?' Maya replies that they are how quickly any ideas could be implemented, how the waiting team would respond to the changes, and how far they would actually improve the quality of the guest experience. Each of the options is then subjected to critical analysis.

Nancy notices that Maya has lost her slumped appearance, in fact seems animated and ready to get going on implementing her favourite solutions.

Now the conversation can progress to assessing what the consequences of implementing any of the changes would be.

Assessing consequences

There are a variety of approaches you can use at this stage. The simplest is to ask what the upsides and downsides of any individual choice would be. If the coachee hesitates here, and especially if you have your own private doubts about the viability of any of the choices, bear these simple headings in mind and ask questions around them:

- *Time*: How long would it take? What would the short-, medium-, and long-term impact be?
- *Money*: What would it cost? How affordable would it be?
- *People*: What resistance might it meet? Who, exactly, might resist? How would you overcome resistance?
- *Practicality*: How sensible is this idea? How practical is it?
- *Personal impact*: What would you need to do differently? What additional support might you need?
- *Unintended negative consequences*: What secondary consequences might there be? What additional problems might you foresee? What would need to be given up if you followed this solution?

For many managers, the problem they face is staying detached when an employee comes up with an inappropriate choice. The OSCAR model enables you to remain neutral while at the same time ensuring that the employee doesn't make a totally inappropriate choice.

Let's suppose that you are having a coaching conversation with a member of your team who has come to you to complain about another team member. Essentially, it is always better for the two people concerned to sort it out between them, without you having to act as referee and your coaching has been aimed at hoping this will happen. But the complainant is still not happy and is threatening to take the whole issue to your own boss, a tactic that would reflect badly on you and probably on the team member him or herself. In circumstances like this, we recommend:

● staying calm – don't react either angrily or by looking scared
● summarizing – this will give you time to think
● asking – what the upsides and downsides of such a course of action would be.

Kathy manages a team providing IT services to her company. Cassie is one of her direct reports. Cassie has a long standing complaint about her own lack of progress and has just been turned down for promotion by one of Kathy's peers in a different department. In the course of a coaching conversation with Kathy about her career, Cassie threatens to take out a grievance against Kathy's colleague. Kathy knows that the person most likely to be damaged by this is Cassie herself, whose moody nature and habit of criticizing others make her an unpopular team member. Staying imperturbable and neutral she says, 'Yes I can see that this is very frustrating for you. Shall we just explore the option of taking out a grievance?' When Cassie nods, she asks a number of questions in turn:

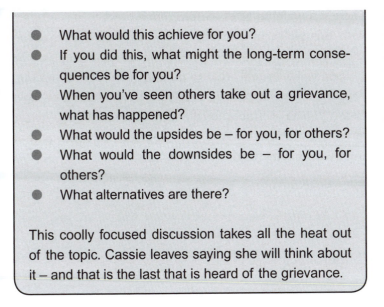

- What would this achieve for you?
- If you did this, what might the long-term consequences be for you?
- When you've seen others take out a grievance, what has happened?
- What would the upsides be – for you, for others?
- What would the downsides be – for you, for others?
- What alternatives are there?

This coolly focused discussion takes all the heat out of the topic. Cassie leaves saying she will think about it – and that is the last that is heard of the grievance.

The next phase is to ask, of all those choices, which one will best move you towards your outcome? This is the action step within the OSCAR model.

Action

Your role here is to get the coachee to name exactly what they are going to do: what, where, when, and how. Your job is to emphasize that carrying out the actions is their responsibility, not yours. The better you have carried out the earlier parts of the coaching conversation the easier this will be, but beware a coachee who:

- becomes vague about timescales
- seems reluctant to commit, says *yes*, but everything about how they look and speak suggests *no*
- looks as if their main aim is to get away from you as quickly as possible.

There is a wide range of reasons that a coachee can struggle with this phase of coaching. They may still feel that the problem is so big that it is out of their control. They may be so used to being told what to do that helplessness kicks in. If you see this happening, first do a double check on how clearly you have established the ideal outcome. If it is unclear or too big, then you may need to double back to this part of the OSCAR framework.

To prevent any of this happening, some good questions are:

> *So let's just summarize who's doing what here. Your tasks are . . .?*

> *What's a reasonable time to come back to me?*

And if you suspect reluctance, never bury it. Raise your concern by saying:

> *I sense a little reluctance here. How committed are you to doing this?*

or

> *How might you sabotage yourself?*

Sometimes reluctance is to do with the belief that even if you take the action, nothing much will change. Another issue may be that something that seems simple enough to you may appear overwhelming to your employee. This is what was happening with Suzie.

Suzie manages several shops in a bakery chain and is being coached by her boss, Phil, over how to address poor performance in one of her shop assistants, a woman who can be brusque with customers, sometimes arrives late and, it has been alleged, sometimes ignores hygiene rules. The agreed action is that Suzie should set up a meeting in her office to tackle the poor performer, but at the Action phase of the conversation Phil notices Suzie's worried frown and lacklustre posture.

'I notice you don't look too keen about this, Suzie'.

'No – really it's OK . . .'.

'Mmm. I'm not convinced. What's going on for you?'

There is a pause. Then slowly Suzie says, 'I just dread this. Some of the evidence is just hearsay. I think she may shout or accuse me of bullying. What if she does?'

Phil, an experienced coach, has met this problem before, so he says: 'Okay. It's perfectly normal to have mixed feelings about this because they are not pleasant conversations to have.'

This is a valuable comment because it normalizes the mixed feelings. He then suggests that he and Suzie should rehearse the conversation. He does not call this 'role play' as he knows the label might put Suzie off, but that is what it is. Phil takes the 'part' of the under-performing shop assistant while Suzie 'plays' herself. She is tentative and unclear about her message, so Phil offers her detailed and supportive feedback and then they do the whole thing again.

'That was so different', says Phil. 'You sounded very firm and clear'. He then describes several of Suzie's behaviours, pointing out how they worked with him in his role. Now he repeats the Action phase discussion, satisfied this time that Suzie really does intend to have the conversation and that it will go well.

Sometimes reluctance at the Action phase is caused by a genuine lack of knowledge or skill. Where lack of enthusiasm to take action is still apparent, it is worth exploring whether this is the problem, for instance by asking:

What else do you need to know to deliver on this?

or

How well equipped do you feel to get going here?

Questions like this make it legitimate for the coachee to own up to any skill deficits or ignorance, in which case you may need to do a further mini piece of coaching around whatever emerges.

The role of the coach is to remain neutral for as long as possible through the coaching process. However, the problem for a line manager is that you can never truly be neutral because whatever action your team member takes, the ultimate responsibility lies with you and that is why the Review component of OSCAR is so important.

Review

When the coach and coachee agree to review the action plan, a subtle pressure is conveyed to the coachee that it is not an option to do nothing. It is vital that as a manager-coach you ensure that these reviews are held – otherwise, you will be giving out a strong message that the actions agreed are discretionary. In many organizations, it is often far too easy for the agreed actions to get lost in the allegedly urgent everyday problems of the job. To stop that happening and to ensure that the person being coached prioritizes their agreed actions, it is vital that they commit to taking some action within the immediate future – to develop momentum and maintain motivation.

The Review component of OSCAR allows the line manager to monitor the team member's progress and commitment. This is useful for another reason – namely, that your own boss will want some assurance that you know what is going on in your team. So when your own boss asks you what is happening about a particular issue, you can respond not only by describing the clear agreed actions being taken but also by taking account of all the thinking that has gone into formulating the action plan itself. This is real control rather than the delusional control that so many managers find themselves living with. Regular reviews allow managers to monitor progress and to stay in control of their own department. During the review phase, the questions are:

Where are you on those actions we agreed?

[And if there is lack of progress]

What's the block?

What prevented you from carrying out what we agreed?

How can you take corrective action?

The Review phase is important for the coachee, as it encourages them to think about how they would ideally wish their review to progress. It might well be that they've taken what to them is major action but none of it has moved them towards their outcome. By sitting with the coach or self-reflecting, they can review which actions have worked and why, which haven't and why, and what they are going to do differently for the future.

End the conversation with agreement to meet again to discuss further progress.

Summary

The OSCAR framework is simple to remember and gives you a structure for the coaching conversation. Each phase has its own helpful questions and will enable you to guard against asking a good question too soon (or too late) as well as ensuring that you do not miss out some vital phase of the process. The question now is to put it all into action – including in some of the most challenging situations a boss can face, for instance as part of performance management, the focus of our next chapter.

OSCAR IN ACTION

In this chapter, we look at a number of common managerial puzzles, including how you manage under-performance, and offer ideas on how coaching can be an effective alternative to more traditional solutions.

In the current climate of recession and severe pressure on costs, there is strong scrutiny of headcount. Every job is a cost to the organization and has to add value to the bottom line. If it does not, then either the person or the job will be eliminated. So as a boss, your role is to create the engagement (Chapter 2) that is the result of high levels of motivation and then to monitor how the team and the individuals inside it are doing against the standards that are necessary for the organization to thrive.

In all the scenarios that follow in this chapter, beware of assuming that the problem is always with the other person. There may indeed be serious performance issues, but it is always worth asking yourself what your own responsibility has been, or even if the problem is actually yours and is nothing much to do with the apparently under-performing team member. For instance, the following are common contributory factors:

- making a mistake at selection and appointing the wrong person
- leaving it far too late to offer the person the feedback that might have set them on the right track
- being unclear about what you expect from them
- never checking how they are getting on with their tasks or asking them what help they need from you
- expecting too much given the resources available to them
- having a personal style that makes it difficult for people to connect with you
- making them the source of the problem when in fact they are merely the last person in a chain of poor management and it was impossible for them to have succeeded.

This is why as well as offering people feedback on how they are doing, you should ask *them* for feedback on how they feel you are managing them (see p. 137). If there are problems on either side, then you have frequent opportunities to spot them and to agree how they should be addressed. Coaching is a low-cost and efficient way to do all of this. The more frequent and informal the coaching conversations are, the less you will need to rely on the clumsy, inefficient, and discredited approach of the annual performance appraisal (p. 24).

The Performance Wheel

The Performance Wheel is an attractive aid to such conversations (see Figure 7.1). It is a visual tool, thus making it easy to use and understand at a glance. You start with a blank wheel and label the eight spokes to capture the essence of the job. Some helpful ones are: Decision-making, Personal Effectiveness, Relationship Building, Customer Service, Administration, Internal Communication, Problem Resolution, and Teamwork. As a team, decide what constitutes excellence (i.e. a score of 10) in each area. Make the point that no one is ever excellent in every area.

Working with individuals using the wheel

There are two aspects to managing performance: getting the task done and developing each individual so that they maximize their potential. In all the drama of trying to do the first, it is easy to overlook the importance of the second. This is where the Performance Wheel can be very useful.

Score the individual yourself and ask them to complete another one themselves as an assessment of their own

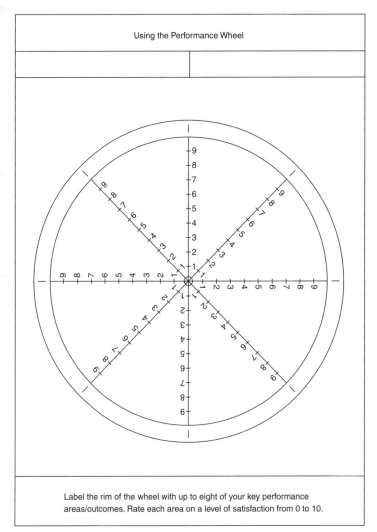

Using the Performance Wheel

Label the rim of the wheel with up to eight of your key performance areas/outcomes. Rate each area on a level of satisfaction from 0 to 10.

Figure 7.1 The Performance Wheel

performance and then to bring it to a development review meeting. Using OSCAR, the Outcome of the meeting is to assess current performance and to agree a way forward. Compare the resulting wheels: this is the Situation phase. Expect to see people over-estimate the excellence of their own performance because most of us do. Discuss your own impressions. Move to Choices and Consequences: what would need to happen to close any gaps? Agree action and then how you will review progress. You should note that focusing on weaknesses can be depressing and that effort spent entirely on trying to remedy weaknesses may result in a mediocre performance all round. A better question is, 'How can we get even better value from your strengths?'

The following example was relayed to us by a senior manager who works in a call centre for a retail bank:

Vicki had qualified as a teacher and wanted to stay near her parents in the north east of England but could not find a teaching job. So she joined our customer care team. She was doing well but in her second year I knew that she was over-qualified for the job. My training as a coach alerted me to the need to have development conversations with my staff and I was soon aware that Vicki was not happy – in fact, she hinted that she was still on the look-out for a teaching post. I wanted to keep her in my team so I booked thirty minutes with her specifically to look at how she felt about the job and to review what we might do. She had filled in the Performance Wheel and so had I. I have customized the wheel to suit our needs, so the areas are now: Interpersonal Empathy; Selling Skills; Verbal Communication; Complaints-handling and Problem-solving; Team Membership; IT Skills; Record-keeping/ Admin; and Product Knowledge (see Figure 7.2).

Her own wheel was more or less exactly the same except that she modestly gave herself 9 where I had given her 10. I am a fan of the idea that we should be looking at strengths rather than deficits, so in the Situation part of the conversation I did ask how she felt

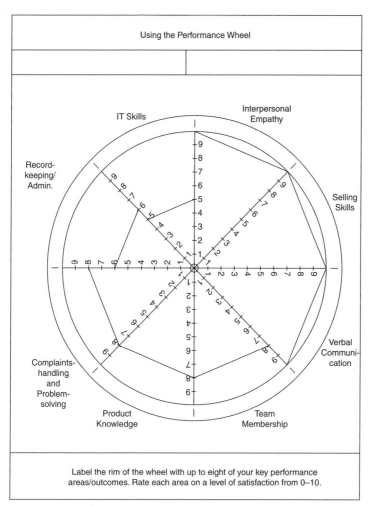

Using the Performance Wheel

Label the rim of the wheel with up to eight of your key performance areas/outcomes. Rate each area on a level of satisfaction from 0–10.

Figure 7.2 Manager's Performance Wheel for Vicky

about the job and it was obvious she felt under-stretched. So I asked her, 'How do you think the organization could make better use of all these strengths?' She immediately replied that she felt she could be an excellent trainer: the stuff she had learnt in her teaching qualification was all relevant, she knew the job inside out, and had that 'development itch'; and she could see how newcomers and existing staff could benefit from specific types of tailored training rather than the generic courses we were running. I asked her to write me a proposal (the Action phase) and I'm happy to say that shortly afterwards she was attached to our training team on a six-month trial where she did very well indeed. Her long-term aim is to go freelance and I feel I can support her in this, but in the meantime we are getting excellent value from her enthusiasm and talent.

Speed coaching: five minutes in the corridor

Coaching is not necessarily a special activity that needs intricate planning and a carefully negotiated date in the diary. It can be a brief five-minute exchange in the corridor or while you are waiting for a meeting to start. The typical scenario here is that you are asked a single question by a team member. The temptation is to offer advice although the person is perfectly capable of answering the question him or herself. They may be looking for reassurance that some proposed action meets with your approval, they may be worried about a sudden problem or may be looking to delegate the problem upwards to you because they are frightened about dealing with it themselves.

Here is how it might go. A team member sees you helping yourself to a cup of coffee while people are gathering before the start of a meeting. She announces, looking a little apprehensive, that there is a difficulty with hitting an important deadline on a project in which you are both involved. What does she want from you? There are several possibilities: reassurance that the deadline can slip, the hope that you will take it over and relieve her of the responsibility, the chance to offer

You say	Your mental dialogue
Mmm . . . Sounds tricky	I need to offer her some rapport here and give her my full attention even though I was hoping to glance at my papers for this meeting, but this sounds like the priority
What do you need from me – I'm aware we've only got five minutes before the meeting starts?	Need to get the Outcome clear and to make it clear time is short
[The team member pauses for a moment and says, 'I need to run my ideas past you']	
So the situation is that we might miss that deadline. What's behind that?	Need to move to S – Situation
[The team member gives you a quick run down on the cause – an equipment breakdown – but also hints at a longer-term safety issue]	
So what are your options here? And what choices do you have?	We're at C (Choices and Consequences) now and I need to make sure I ask her for upsides and downsides and don't overlook the safety issue in a future conversation
[The team member quickly outlines two possible courses of action, briefly describing why she prefers Option A to Option B. You nod wisely while she is talking, encouraging her to continue without interrupting. The conversation then moves to the Action and Review phases]	
Yes, I agree, Option A sounds best to me too. What's your next step?	Make sure she tells me when this is going to happen and how she will get back to me to report on progress, and get a meeting in the diary to look at the safety problem

you her own solutions. You have no means of knowing, but you do know that this is an opportunity for coaching.

This conversation took 4 minutes and 30 seconds. It is over by the time the Chair taps a glass and starts the meeting.

Speed coaching is a good solution when the problem is relatively simple or is part of an ongoing dialogue. In fact, when coaching does become your default way of managing, long coaching sessions become less and less vital because coaching is knitted into every conversation you have with each member of your team.

Planned coaching with a willing, self-aware coachee

This is the sunny, easy side of coaching. Use it when you have a star or promising performer who has more potential than they are currently fulfilling. This could be because they are young and relatively inexperienced or because they have somehow got stuck in a rut job-wise and may lack some essential skill that would fit them for promotion. The coachee is already aware that this is the case and is eager for help. So the coaching conversation might be an informal one-to-one, a formal part of a personal development plan or it could be one slice of a performance review. A few brief questions using the OSCAR framework are usually all you will need – in effect, the coachee coaches him or herself.

Here is how it was applied by one of the managers we trained. He works for a restaurant chain specializing in budget meals for families.

The company makes it clear when they take you on as a manager that they expect you to stay three to four years and then move on, as the hierarchy is very flat. There's an executive team, a small group of regional managers and then the restaurant managers. The restaurant manager job is a good career move for a keen young graduate in their second job after university. We do invest in people's development as we have an Academy where people go on a series of day courses to hone their management skills. Daisy had been in the job nearly three years, she'd taken full advantage of the Academy experience and it was clear that she was outstanding in the job. She knew a promotion was unlikely but was keen to have a go. In one of our regular reviews, we agreed to explore this. We started with me checking her understanding on the promotion situation. She was very realistic about this. At the Outcome stage of our conversation, we agreed easily that this was 'Find strategies for increasing my chances of impressing the Chief Executive as a potential Regional Manager'. In the Situation part of the conversation, we reviewed her current levels of experience and skill. This revealed that she knew her profile company-wide was too low and that she was a little too modest for her own good. We then discussed the C: Choices and Consequences. After a mini-brainstorm (see p. 150), she came up with three ideas: offer to run a special customer survey to identify what kids were actually eating in the restaurants; make a presentation to the Exec Team on another highly relevant topic at the next opportunity; organize a special fund-raising event for Shelter, our charity of choice. I did double check that this would not mean taking on too much but she fizzes with energy and we easily agreed the Actions, which were that she would carry out the survey and make the presentation, etc. Then we

> agreed how we would review the actions, for instance, run the draft of the survey past me in two weeks' time, get a date into the Executive team agenda immediately and give me some draft ideas for the fund-raiser within a week. Really, all the ideas came from her. All I did was ask a few questions. Eighteen months later she was our youngest Regional Manager.

Planned coaching with an unaware coachee

Here we enter the territory that many managers dread. Someone in your team appears to be unaware of how unacceptable their behaviour is. Both you and others have dropped hints, but the behaviour continues. It is not yet a make or break issue, but it could be and you have to intervene before a problem grows into a mess that could damage you and have serious consequences for the team member.

You will call the meeting. You will also set the Outcome at the first part of the meeting. Whatever the context, the outcome will be a variant of 'Get X to understand that there is a problem'. The traditional ways of doing this are to state it bluntly or to wrap it up in so much waffle that the other person is confused about what you are trying to say. By taking it in stages so that your main aim is to raise awareness of the problem, you increase the chances that the coachee will be able to accept and act on whatever emerges. The coaching way is to be clear what the goal for the meeting is, but to make sure that you get the person's own view of whatever is going on, adjusting your style to the other person. Some people can take more directness than others. Here is an account of how one meeting of this kind went, described by a manager who runs a team of journalists.

I'd always had a few doubts about Lee, but he was keen, intelligent, hardworking, with a nose for a story and the ability to dig for it – and had a good degree in journalism from a university I respect and some impressive track record on a local radio station. The fact that he seemed a little abrasive should have alerted me, but I appointed him. We work in an open plan area and after a bit people began coming to me saying he was rude, over-competitive, was hugging stories to himself when he should have been working collaboratively. But even worse was that he was aggressive with members of the public and contacts. It was all perfectly visible and audible. I could hear him shouting or sounding irritable on the phone several times a day. When I learnt the OSCAR framework, I could see how useful it would be. I called him in and said very directly that my Outcome for the meeting was to get him to understand that he had a problem and that therefore I did too because I was responsible for our output and the behaviour of my team. I stopped at this point and asked him how he saw it. He looked startled and a bit angry and said that he thought he was one of the most hardworking people in the newsroom and everything he did was in the interests of getting a good story. I agreed that he was indeed hardworking and said that I admired his diligence and drive, calmly summarized what he'd said and then went on to 'S': Situation. I reminded him of our agreed values: courtesy, friendliness, diligence, persistence, truth. I used the rules of feedback to describe what I'd seen and heard myself and said, 'Lee, I heard you on the phone yesterday to X (a local politician) when you said [. . .] I cringed as I imagined what it would be like to be on the receiving end of it. It seemed to me that you were actually arguing with him – and that's not the behaviour we expect, not least because it's unlikely to get you the story you want'.

At this stage I stopped and was aware that I needed to explore what was going on for him, including his beliefs about what was appropriate and what wasn't. This was interesting: at first he was his usual strident self, but then he calmed down. He told me that he felt he always had to be 'Number 1' and that you had to confront people to get them to tell the truth. He believed that 'politicians always lie'. We had a long discussion about this where I challenged most of these beliefs. It was clear to me that he thought his own behaviour was just 'direct', 'telling it as it is', and had no idea that other people saw this as aggression. He attributed success in his career thus far as evidence that it worked, whereas I had to say that I thought any success had been despite this behaviour, not because of it. I told him that shouting and belligerence were totally unacceptable for any member of my team. I was aware I was still at 'S', and asked him what he thought would happen if he did nothing. That was the turning point. I could see from his reply that the idea dawned on him for the first time that his job could be at risk despite all his many good qualities. The rest was easy. At C: Choices and Consequences, we explored a number of options, most of them offered by him, and agreed that he could return to me the following week for some coaching on how he could moderate his typical responses to frustration. Action and Review were that he and I would jointly monitor his behaviour during the next few days and after that.

I was aware that I had some responsibility here as I had let it go on too long without intervening, hoping

> that he might realize himself from colleague feedback that he was in trouble. So I had action points as well as he.

Note that Lee's boss wisely realized that such deeply rooted ways of behaving are unlikely to be changed in a single conversation. He understood that Lee would need close supervision with constant support and further coaching. Whether or not this will have a positive ending will depend on how far Lee is able to moderate behaviour that has become second nature to him and which he believes, wrongly, has been responsible for his success.

What happens if the coachee's suggested choices seem inadequate?

Depending on the coachee's level of unawareness, his or her suggested solutions may seem inadequate to you. The traditional way of tackling this would be to argue and to revert to telling. This may achieve short-term results but is unlikely to be effective in the longer term as it will create resentment or dependency – or possibly both. Coaching offers an alternative that allows the coachee to stay motivated, to maintain self-respect, and for you to continue to ask for what you want. If none of the suggested choices seems robust, and the coachee appears to be ignoring some downside that seems obvious to you, then the best tactic is to voice your concerns:

I can't see how that option is going to meet the need to [be calmer on the phone/deal with customer feedback, etc.]

If further discussion still does not seem to satisfy you, then again, say why and ask for additional options:

I'm still not convinced. How can you reassure me that this is going to answer the need to [do whatever is necessary to solve the problem]?

To use OSCAR in this type of scenario, these are the guidelines:

- Act promptly when you see behaviour that runs counter to agreed values or when performance appears to be below standard.
- Ask for the meeting and set aside enough time in private.
- Take control of the Outcome and Situation stage, remembering that the coachee appears to be unaware that there is a problem. Your role is to raise their awareness.
- Listen patiently as you explore what is going on for them. Remember it could be anything: events in their private life, beliefs they hold, lack of knowledge, a failure of training – and equally importantly, some deficit on your own part, such as failure to communicate a key policy.
- At the Choices and Consequences stage, the conversation becomes more collaborative. Encourage the coachee to establish their own ideas about options and to choose whichever seem most appropriate.
- Be prepared to challenge any of the options for action that do not quell your own anxieties.
- There will be a role for you at the Action and Review stages. If you have contributed yourself to the development of the problem, you need to acknowledge it. The coachee may well need support and further input from you, or maybe some additional training. Never end this kind of meeting without a tightly defined agreement about how you will monitor progress.

Planned coaching with an acknowledged poor performer

The scenario here is that your team member is already aware that there is a problem with their performance. You have already had the uncomfortable feedback conversation and they have acknowledged the difficulty. It is usually worth giving a coaching approach a try rather than swinging straight into disciplinary action. The only difference with the previous scenario is that the emphasis in the conversation is on reinforcing the evidence of under-performance, drawing this out from the coachee. The emphasis at the Choices and Consequence stage is on joint solution-hunting and with even more emphasis on the Action and Review phases. Here is an example, written by a manager in the voluntary sector who acknowledges her surprise at the power of this approach.

Before learning about OSCAR and coaching I was impatient with poor performers. The charity sector is under so much pressure now that we can't carry passengers. Suzanne runs our major events among other tasks and her performance was well under par, although she is a pleasant young woman with a lot of excellent qualities in other respects. The worst example and the one that brought it to a head was that we had a big reception at Tower Bridge for our funders and sponsors and so much went embarrassingly wrong. The senior politician who was giving the main speech wasn't welcomed properly, the champagne wasn't chilled, the guest list was inaccurate . . . it went on and on and it reflected very badly on me – in fact, the Chair of Trustees scowled his way through the whole thing and gave me a humiliating dressing-down as soon as it was over and implied I should get rid of her. But thanks to my coaching training I felt I had to give her one last chance.

I allowed thirty minutes for the first meeting and used it to underline the feedback. She totally accepted that she had made a number of mistakes and we drew up a service recovery plan that included a graceful letter of apology to the politician and to the Chair. But that left the whole question of why it had happened in the first place.

In the second meeting, I asked her to come with suggestions. So we began with a jointly agreed Outcome, which was 'How we can restore mutual confidence that you can do the events management part of the job?' In the Situation part of the discussion, I used the Performance Wheel as a focus to establish what good performance would look like and asked her to fill it in for herself. She marked the Admin 'spoke' at 2 and the Customer Service 'spoke' at 3 (see Figure 7.3). This was the most revealing part of the discussion. I asked her what was standing in the way of this becoming a higher score. I put a lot of effort into maintaining rapport at the same time as being clear that this could become a formal disciplinary matter. It surprised me very much to learn that an inability to type fast and accurately and discomfort with computer software was Suzanne's own diagnosis, along with some mild dyslexia. The laborious time all of this was taking was sabotaging her well-meant attempts to give good service to customers.

She had felt ashamed of this and had concealed it from everyone. After that it was easy. Without any prompting from me, she suggested an intensive touch-typing course and asked if we could fund a one-to-one tutor to learn how to use Word – for example, for mail merge. This was cheap at the price. The dyslexia issue was harder but she came up with a few ideas on that too. In a nutshell, she stayed, ran the next big event impeccably, with lots of coaching-style reporting-in to me to check on progress, and I realized that coaching had actually saved us loads of money – the cost of losing her, recruiting a successor, etc., would have been far in excess of the modest cost of her remedial training and the few hours of her and my time that we took on the coaching.

Coaching people with a victim mentality

You may occasionally have to manage someone who is fixed in the role of victim. To deal with it skilfully, you need first to understand that a 'victim mentality' is different from the temporary anguish and helplessness any of us can feel when faced with a sudden traumatic experience, for instance, a profound career setback, the death of a loved one or the diagnosis of a serious illness. However flattened we may feel at the time by these inevitable challenges, most of us will eventually bounce back. This is very different from the mindset of a person whose whole life position is that they are helpless and that other people or events outside of their control are always to blame.

Such people can be tiresome colleagues, a draining presence, always looking for cheap sympathy, seeing the pessimistic side of everything and eagerly searching for reinforcement from others that their own views are justified. And if you are apparently the source of their frustration, then you can expect

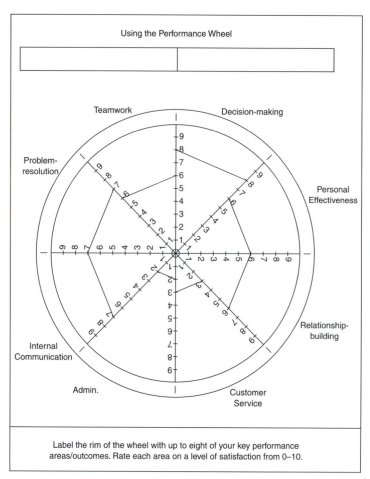

Figure 7.3 Suzanne's self-assessed Performance Wheel

blaming statements aimed at you, the purpose of which is to induce guilt and to keep you at bay. This book is not the place to go into the reasons such mindsets develop, except to say that they are always the result of misguided parenting. People who are fixed in the role of victim are terrified of taking responsibility for themselves. Their anger and disappointment turn inwards. Privately they believe themselves to be worthless and it is too frightening to contemplate how they might address whatever they imagine their deficits to be. It is easier to criticize from the sidelines and to assume a 'poor me' attitude.

They will rarely ask you for coaching. However, they will still present you with opportunities to coach. Typical scenarios include a general sense of tragic weariness or else a right-eous and prickly anger:

- coming to complain about someone else; wanting to change the behaviour of others without being willing to change their own
- making excuses for performance failures by putting the blame on circumstances or other people
- feeling persecuted
- whipping up discontent about necessary changes
- constant harking back to the past and how others made mistakes that were fatally damaging or else to a time when allegedly everything was rosy
- black-and-white thinking about people and events.

You are not a therapist (and by the way such people rarely opt for or stick at therapy because it is too challenging), so your task is not to change their mindset, only to deal with its consequences.

Julia manages an admin team of nine. Mostly everyone gets on well, but Terry, one of the two men in the team, seems to have difficulty fitting in. His work is mediocre: he often misses deadlines and makes clumsy mistakes with the detail of data entry that is essential in the admin role. Colleagues have frequently had to rescue his work and pick up complaints made by their internal clients. Terry often invites himself into Julia's office, apparently to seek her help and advice. He tells her that his colleagues tease him, treat him differently because he's a man, give him all the worst jobs, leave him out of social events, and that he looks to her to make things better for him. Would she, for instance, talk to Elizabeth about her loud, grating voice and awful jokes? He makes vague threats about lodging a grievance for sexual harassment. Julia dreads his visits. They leave her feeling exhausted and snappy.

Julia is then a participant on a coaching training course commissioned by her company, during which she is taught to recognize patterns of flawed thinking in herself and others. She sees now that Terry is really using these discussions as a way to try to force her to solve his problems by intervening and by putting responsibility for his poor performance on to others. If she carries on doing this, with tactful little hints to the admin team about behaving nicely to one another, or reminding them about company policy on sexual harassment, she now realizes that this just reinforces Terry's self-awarded victim status. Julia needs to investigate Terry's allegations and when she does, she is quickly satisfied that they are entirely without foundation.

What do you do if you are in Julia's position? OSCAR will still work, but you will have to seize the chance to shape and then change the agenda at the Outcome stage. The coachee will be coming to complain about others, and may say that what they want as an outcome is for you to rap the knuckles of their annoying colleagues. Instead of falling into this trap, it will be better to restate it as 'Improve relationships with colleagues'.

At the Situation stage, you will be alert to the give-away phrases:

- 'If only they hadn't/wouldn't . . .'.
- Generalizations suggesting that other people are mostly getting things wrong around this person. 'Everything would be fine if only . . . They always . . .'.
- A complete absence of any sense that we all choose our life paths, including how we respond to others.
- Anecdotes, often reaching back years, into other people's faults.

Tactics that work

Julia should listen carefully and summarize accurately, refraining from getting drawn into the debate about who is right and who is wrong at this stage. Feedback in the here-and-now (see p. 136) is probably her most potentially powerful tactic. So Julia might say, calmly, kindly and thoughtfully:

> *Terry, I notice that while we've been talking you've only told me about what the others have said and done and it's all been negative [she gives some direct quotes].*

She could then follow this with a challenge

> *In any set of relationships there are two sides, and I'm wondering what your own contribution has been?*

or

> *I wonder how this would look from the other side? What do you think they might say about you?*

Terry's most likely response will be defensive. He might go on the attack, blaming Julia for her failure to be 'a proper manager'. Julia needs to stay steady and calm when this happens, seeing it as part of the way Terry has skilfully built defences around himself for so many years. Her best bet will be to continue with her observational feedback:

So Terry, I notice that, again, you're putting the responsibility on to others. I haven't yet heard you say what you might be contributing.

At this stage Julia can say that she knows about the missed deadlines and data entry mistakes, giving him the factual evidence she has collected. The typical victim coachee will now adopt two possible behaviours: flouncing out (and in its extreme form, claiming to have been bullied and going off sick with alleged 'stress') or collapsing into tears, both recognizably victim behaviours. Let's assume he stays, or if he does not, he will eventually be obliged to reappear to continue the conversation at some other time. This is where the two C's of OSCAR come into their own. What are his ideas about choices? Which will have the best chances of meeting the original Outcome – in this case, to improve relationships all round? Julia needs to be aware that underneath his aggressive whining and complaining, Terry is a vulnerable human being whose instinct will be to protect himself by demanding changes from others, including herself. Her skill as a coach will be in pushing Terry for suggestions about how his own behaviour needs to change, possibly quoting the useful old cliché that 'behaviour breeds behaviour' – in other words, the behaviour we display has a profound influence on the behaviour we get back – or yet another equally useful cliché, that 'If you go on doing what you've always done, you'll get what you've always got'. With people like Terry, it is sensible to expect only modest improvement at first, but with a great deal of support at the Action and Review stages he may well be able to bring his work up to the required standard. And who knows, experiencing the success that comes at last from taking responsibility, he may even be able to change at least some of the mental habits of a lifetime.

Note that this approach will not be appropriate if what you uncover when you investigate allegations about bullying, sexist or racist behaviour is that the allegations are essentially true.

Coaching is not the answer to every performance problem: sometimes the issue is too extreme and the only solution is a disciplinary process. We discuss this in the final chapter.

Summary

The OSCAR framework is a flexible tool that can be used in a variety of day-to-day management challenges, whether it is for a fleeting five-minute corridor discussion, dealing with poor performers or using it for planned development conversations about career. The Performance Wheel is a visual approach to discussing performance and can be customized to suit particular jobs. Using the OSCAR approach emphasizes that coaching is not the soft option that some people may think. It firmly obliges staff members to reconsider their own performance and development and uses the kind of coaching approach that makes change more likely than traditional methods of performance management.

The OSCAR framework is easy to use for one-to-one coaching but it has many other applications. The next chapter is about how OSCAR can also be a vital tool for day-to-day meetings that are often difficult to handle, as well as in managing change successfully.

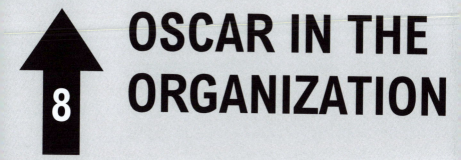

8 OSCAR IN THE ORGANIZATION

So far, we have addressed coaching individuals, but coaching has many applications beyond one-to-one conversations. In this chapter, we show how it can be a powerful way of improving team functioning, creating better meetings, and of managing change in organizations generally.

The impact on teams

What happens when coaching affects a whole team? This senior manager describes what happened when an entire department in a Housing Association embraced coaching. It is an example of how coaching can percolate with profit through several levels in the organization, affecting not only how performance is managed but how meetings are run, quickly proving that it has bottom-line benefit.

In the Housing Maintenance department there were two team leaders who were significantly underperforming, as were their sections. There was a culture of blame, low trust, an unwillingness to take responsibility, and a lack of ownership. The impact on the staff they managed was poor performance, low output, and unacceptable standards. This resulted in a high number of complaints from tenants and from the other departments in the organization with whom they had to work. We appointed a new manager, Matt, and made it clear that it was his job to sort it out but he soon found he was spending far too much time dealing with day-to-day operational issues. His team leaders were refusing to take ownership for their performance and continually tried to refer everything upwards. The directors had actually considered outsourcing the whole section.

Unfortunately, Matt's go-for-it approach upset people and I sent him on the 'manager-as-coach' programme. He started to use a coaching style of management with his team leaders. I also coached Matt to help him stop just giving solutions to his direct reports and in turn he coached them through the decision-making process with the use of the OSCAR model. He also used this model to frame discussions and used it explicitly for problem-solving at team and other meetings. Within two months one team leader was doing fantastically well, productivity had increased, and staff were no longer referring upwards for decisions; instead, they were responding directly and effectively to tenants and to other departments. Staff motivation increased and sickness absence levels dramatically decreased. Staff were also offering great suggestions for improvement and efficiency, most of which were implemented.

The other team leader remained a sceptic until the moment when Matt coached him through managing the consequences of one of his poorer decisions. Previously the department's practice would have been to tell him off and use him as a scapegoat. This person is now considered to be a high performer within the organization. The director concerned acknowledged Matt's success at a board meeting when he reported on how all targets had been met and exceeded, and on the high levels of tenant satisfaction.

This department now has one of the lowest levels of sickness absence in the organization and its 'rework' level is negligible.

Using OSCAR for meetings

How people can hate meetings – and with good reason. Meetings jokes abound:

Meetings are events that take minutes and waste hours.

There are two kinds of work in organizations: going to meetings and taking messages for people who are in meetings.

Message from senior to junior management: we are going to have to continue meeting until we discover why no work is being done.

All of this is especially true of those meandering routine meetings where the purpose is obscure, the agenda is vague, and people show their lack of commitment by sending a 'deputy', or by arriving late and leaving early. Another meeting then has to be scheduled to make the decisions that were not made at the original meeting, often because the people with decision-making authority had avoided being present on the grounds that the meeting was likely to be boring or pointless. The OSCAR model can help because it provides the structure that is missing from many meetings. Productive meetings are enjoyable, build relationships, save time, and produce better quality decisions. Taking a coaching approach, facilitating rather than directing, makes it clear that you expect everyone to play their part.

When planning a meeting, ask yourself:

- Do you really need this meeting at all?
- What do you hope to achieve as an outcome?
- Who needs to be there?
- What will they expect and need from the meeting?
- What do they need to know or prepare in advance?
- What is the maximum time it needs to take?

Meetings are valuable when you need to review where you would like to be (the longer-term outcome) against the present, decide how to close the gap, agree action and review.

OSCAR is equally valuable as a framework for meetings, where the manager takes what becomes a group-coach role, helping to make meetings more productive and enjoyable for everyone who attends.

Here is how the OSCAR framework can be used for an hour-long meeting to address a specific issue:

O	*Outcome* Establish the agenda What do we need to achieve from this meeting?	5 minutes
S	*Situation* Review actions agreed at last meeting Where are we now? What's the gap between the ideal and the present?	15 minutes
C	*Choices and Consequences* (Options) What options do we have for moving forward? Taking each in turn, what are their plusses and minuses?	30 minutes
A	*Action* What are our agreed action points? Who is doing what? By what time?	5 minutes
R	*Review* How has this meeting been? Did we achieve our objectives? How could we improve the quality of this meeting another time?	5 minutes

The question of how to facilitate such meetings, dealing with the sometimes eccentric and challenging behaviour of group members is beyond our brief in this book,[1] but the OSCAR framework provides a firm structure and reduces the chances of a meeting getting out of control or becoming just another pointless aspect of organizational bureaucracy. Here is how Amanda, a senior manager in the NHS and a convert to this approach, describes the benefit:

People in the NHS can be very cavalier about attending meetings because meetings generally have a bad name, and for good reason because so many are badly run or just unnecessary, so people regard attendance as optional, even when the topic is actually important. I realized that in my own meetings I was allowing the same thing to happen. The very worst aspect was that at the end of the meetings I was the only one with action points and I began to dread the meetings knowing I'd be walking away with yet another huge list. People were avoiding responsibility because I was behaving as if I had to make all the decisions and not using a coaching approach. I saw that the same coaching principles could be applied to a group meeting as to one-to-one sessions. I started with team meetings and sent everyone an email saying I recognized that the quality of our meetings had been below standard but that there would be a new regime from now on. I said I expected everyone to attend and contribute, and I attached a simple grid explaining how OSCAR worked. I made it clear that the action points would be shared and would arise from a proper discussion on the options. Just devoting a few minutes at the end to reviewing the meeting itself was transformational. If people said, 'I didn't like x or y thing', or 'We didn't discuss my issue', I would say, very politely, 'So what prevented you raising that during the meeting?' Knowing that they would be asked this soon meant that people joined in the agenda-setting process. It really helped to make it clear that we would start the next meeting with a review of action points since the last one and that anyone who had done nothing would look a bit pathetic. We've gone from three-hour to one-hour meetings and get a more or less full house every time. Decision-making has been driven down to its proper level and altogether we are far more productive.

Coaching and change in organizations

We all know that change is unstoppable and that its pace is increasing, driven mostly by forces we barely understand and cannot control: the rise of the 'tiger economies', the crisis in the western banking system, climate change, depletion of the planet's natural resources, social upheaval, wars, population movements, technological inventions, and many more. So there is no way that any organization or indeed any individual can hope to continue jogging along peacefully doing now what they were doing even a few years ago. Change can be exhilarating and frightening; sometimes it is both at once.

This will affect you, the people you manage, and the entire organization in which you work. As a coach to your team, change will challenge you constantly. For instance, here are some common scenarios:

Senior people have decided on the future direction of the organization. This involves an ambitious programme of expansion globally. There are interesting prospects of promotion for you but all will probably involve a change of country and therefore upheaval for you and your family.

As a result of a drop in profit and a consequent cost-cutting programme, you have to make a member of your team redundant, knowing that as the breadwinner in her family this will cause her immense pain and stress.

A merger means new systems including new IT programs. It feels like it was only a few months ago that you eventually grasped how to use the last new system; now you and your team will have to do it all over again.

Your firm has decided to sell its car park. Your journey to work will now have to be by public transport, adding another two hours to your working day. Some of your team have said that this could mean they will have to leave.

The government has introduced new targets in your sector and these mean an inbox full of forms to fill in and data to gather. This will take many hours of your time and still leaves you with your basic job to do.

You have been promoted. You imagined that the new job would be just like the old one but on a bigger scale. This turns out to be untrue. The new job does not seem to need the skills you acquired so steadily in your old job but it does need a whole new set of skills, all of them unfamiliar and with little time in which to acquire them.

Continuous improvement

As well as the challenges of full-on change, all organizations have to accept that to keep their customers, they need to commit to continuous improvement. As fast as some needed improvement has been made, another is necessary. You can see this very clearly in the retail sector, especially with supermarkets. An initiative by, say, Waitrose, to introduce an upmarket range of ready meals is instantly visible to all their competitors, so Marks & Spencer will probably produce a similar idea – or vice versa. Tesco's membership scheme will vie with Iceland's similar product. One retailer may boast of taking dangerous 'trans-fats' and high levels of salt out of their chilled products but it will only be a matter of months before their competitors are doing the same. What was extraordinary service by one retailer when it was first introduced soon becomes standard throughout the industry as others quickly copy it. It has been estimated that it takes less than a year for a genuine innovation in one supermarket company to become standard in all of them. This is also true in the technology sector where, for instance, Apple has a legendary reputation for daring product launches and rapidly developed new versions of already successful products. So the creation of the iPAD, a tablet computer, was initially derided as just being some eccentric kind of giant smartphone, but within its first year it had sold several million units, fast followed by new versions and leaving startled rivals with the difficult task of catching up.

The speed of change means that staff also have to be speedy. They need to be nimble: quick learners, ready to ask themselves difficult questions, and constantly looking for ways to beat the next wave of innovation, even when they appear to be already ahead of the game. Managers who can demonstrate that they can coach their staff through successive waves of change will always be in demand: it is one of the most desirable and universally transportable skills you can have.

There are many different models of change and one of the simplest and most helpful is the change and competence curve (Figure 8.1). It assumes that in dealing with change we pass through four typical stages, the middle two of which are inherently stressful because they involve anxiety about being able to cope. You should note that stress caused by anxiety is now the single largest contributor to workplace absence. During periods of rapid change, anxiety is heightened – thus causing increased stress. There is growing

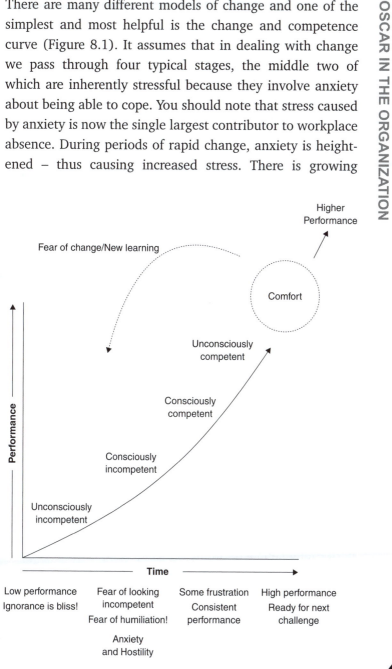

Figure 8.1 The change and competence curve

evidence to suggest that a coaching style of leadership and management can be a highly effective way of reducing stress during times of change.

In this model, change has four phases: unconscious incompetence, conscious incompetence, conscious competence, and unconscious competence. Performance is driven up by moving quickly up the curve. When you reach the apparent comfort zone of conscious competence, there is hidden danger. The very success of a company means that its achievements become visible to competitors and it may be relatively easy for them to replicate the formula at lower prices, thus stealing some of the market. This is why so many companies appear prone to sudden failures when apparently at the peak of their success. Unconscious competence has become complacency and with it goes a renewed fear of change.

Effective organizations recognize the hidden danger of the unconsciously competent stage and use a coaching approach to help high-performing individuals and teams identify what it is they are doing well and deliberately encourage a return to the consciously competent stage as a way of looking for further improvement. In this way, continuous improvement becomes a way of life.

It is worth noting that this is what all top sports coaches do – they encourage their coachees to watch videos of their performance to help them build on their successes and address any minor imperfections. In our opinion, all high-performing people naturally self-coach and constantly move from the unconsciously competent down to the consciously competent stage so that they can improve their performance. A manager who can help their team do the same will ensure that the team and its individual members see change as a positive and constant state, rather than a stress-inducing activity that has been forced on them.

Stages on the change and competence curve

One common feature of change is that as a manager you may typically be at least one stage ahead of your staff. This is because you will probably have had advance warning of change and will have had more time to consider the implications. That said, all of these stages will apply to you too.

Stage 1: Unconscious incompetence

The first stage is characterized by unawareness of incompetence, and performance is low. Feelings at this stage are neutral because ignorance is innocence. Organizations that allow their employees to stay at this stage will ultimately fail.

Your coaching role at this stage: to alert staff to what could happen or is actually about to happen. Typical reactions may include head-in-sand responses such as 'we've seen things like this before and it won't affect me', or a naive belief that the old skills will still be good enough. Don't be afraid to challenge. Tactics that might work include:

- talking about competitors and their successes
- asking frontline staff to share their experience with customers/users: this will often reveal complaints about costs or quality compared with those of competitors
- showing staff candid figures that reveal uncomfortable trends
- emphasizing the right of regulators to impose change
- raising awareness of the likely negative consequences if the organization does nothing
- reassuring staff that there will be support at the stages to come
- creating a sense of pleasurable excitement about what change might achieve

● promising people that they will be consulted and involved – and meaning it!

Stage 2: Conscious incompetence

The change has happened and you are faced with inability to catch up quickly enough: ignorance or lack of skill – or both. The task of learning seems enormous. Others may appear to be doing better and you look at them with envy. Shock, despair, fear, humiliation, a wish to return to the apparently golden past and the feeling of never being able to learn or adjust will typically accompany this phase. There may be a lot of blaming, a high level of sickness absence and unhelpful rumours may abound.

Your coaching role at this stage: coaching can be critically important here. Make regular progress checks. Hold open meetings where it is okay to ask any question and answer it respectfully, however aggressively asked or challenging the question seems. Share whatever information you have and even if there is no new information, tell staff that this is the case. Encourage staff to confide in you on a one-to-one basis; reassure them that their feelings are normal, offer them time and encouragement, make training available if appropriate. Some staff may try to protect themselves by deriding the changes and by criticizing you or your boss: don't over-react, especially if you have only just left Stage 2 yourself and are having your own battles with confidence. Organizations that allow their employees to stay at this stage will ultimately face burn-out and failure, so it is important to keep going. Remember the comforting old saying that 'everything feels like a failure in the middle'.

Where major reorganization is part of the change process, staff may have to go through painful assessment processes and compete for what they see as their 'own' jobs. This is not always well handled. In one such organization, as a result of a merger, a distinguished senior manager had to compete for the job along with two equally distinguished peers. The invitation letter to the interview and selection centre began 'Dear XX'. It had apparently been signed by an extremely senior figure in his sector. As he said, 'Could she not even be bothered to read through the letter and to spot this rudeness?' Where staff have to be made redundant, offer them your own time to coach them through their next career steps as well as making sure that there is organization-sponsored help available for them such as outplacement services or career workshops on how to write a CV and get through a job interview successfully. Support the people who will be staying, looking out for 'survivor syndrome', the guilt and discomfort survivors can feel at keeping their jobs when well-liked colleagues have lost out.

Stage 3: Conscious competence

You may have learnt whatever the new skill is, but you have to make a conscious effort to manage it. It feels clunky, you can't relax, you feel ill at ease, and think everyone can see how difficult it is for you. You are aware that some of what you are doing is high-level copying because you have yet to customize the skill to your own unique style and this feels stressful.

Your coaching role at this stage: providing reassurance and encouragement to keep going. Tell people that such feelings are normal and that it will get better. Ask them where they are beginning to get enjoyment from their newly found skills. Give high-quality and enthusiastic feedback when you see for yourself that they are doing good work and carefully phrased feedback when you see something that could be improved. Offer people further training if they feel it would help embed the new skills; make it legitimate to discuss how people feel by putting the topic on team meeting agendas. Setting up buddy arrangements can help where people can coach each other. It is only human to want to skip the discomforts of this phase, yearning instead for the instant competence that is not usually possible. Organizations that allow their employees to stay at this stage will create reasonable performance – but will not maximize it.

Stage 4: Unconscious competence

You are good at something and you don't even have to think about it any more because it feels natural. The skill has become second nature and you have created your own style and protocols. If necessary, you could teach others.

Your coaching role at this stage: notice it, comment. Ask, 'Is the organization getting the very best that we could out of the strengths you are showing? How satisfying is it? Where could you be helping others get to the same level?' Encourage people to look outside the organization at what competitors are up to and to look at customer data. Where is the next challenge going to come from? How might you be ready to meet it with new products and services?

Over time, unconscious competence can start to feel a little neutral because it is comfortable. This is the stage where high performance happens. However, if we remain in our comfort zone for too long, we start to experience some negative emotions, and boredom can set in with a corresponding impact on performance. Staying at this level for too long can mean that performance actually starts to drop. At an organizational level, this can be catastrophic, as competitors can overtake and capture market share. When an organization is committed to continuous improvement, this really means that it wants to go beyond the cumulative comfort zones of all the people who work there. Organizations that can achieve this will be the winners in tomorrow's markets.

Summary

Introducing coaching on a wider scale can mean immediate improvements in how a team functions, and the OSCAR model can also be used as a way of planning and running meetings. Major change is now an inevitable part of organization life. The change and competence curve is a helpful way of understanding the psychological impact of change and of using coaching as a vital part of raising performance levels as quickly as possible.

Even if you are the only person in your organization adopting a coaching approach, you will achieve results. But it may feel lonely and you may be conspicuous because your own style of managing will be different from what is happening all around you. For true success, coaching needs to be embedded into the whole organization. This means creating a coaching culture, the subject of our next chapter.

Note

1. For more on these, see *Facilitating Groups* by Jenny Rogers (2010), a practical guide to getting what you need from meetings, including advice on how to deal with nightmare behaviour from group members.

9

CREATING A COACHING CULTURE

There is a sizeable difference between an individual manager using coaching with a team and having a 'coaching culture' in the whole organization. This chapter looks at what it really means in practice to have this desirable state and what you might need to do to achieve it.

It is possible that some companies already have a coaching culture but if they do, we have yet to meet them. What we do know is how many of our client organizations see creating such a culture as a challenging and desirable goal. Most such organizations are realistic, they know this is a journey not a destination, and they know how much effort it is going to take to get there. We hear vague boasts from some organizations whose HR people speak at conferences, alleging that they already have a coaching culture, but actually what they usually mean is something along the following lines:

We do a lot of coaching

We have trained lots of our line managers in how to coach

Our senior managers all have external coaches

HR is keen on coaching

None of these amounts to having a coaching culture, although each might be a sign that you are on your way.

What is culture?

The concept of culture in organizations come from the work of social anthropologists – people who study whole societies, originally 'primitive' societies, very different from the traditional western view of the world, but now applied to societies everywhere. Why is it that people behave so differently in different countries? And why is it that there are no fundamental values common to the human species as a whole? For instance, the mother–child bond is considered sacred in most human societies, but there are some in which infants are routinely murdered, for instance baby girls in societies where males are valued over females. The word 'culture' describes long-lasting beliefs passed from one generation to another that affect the way people behave. There are radical differences in behaviour between one organization and another, just as there are in whole societies. Culture in organizations is usually described as 'the way we do things around here'. Culture can take one of two forms:

- *Visible culture*: dress; length of working day; where and what people eat; physical environment.
- *Deeper culture*: values and beliefs that may not always be readily described.

There is a strong cause-and-effect relationship between whether or not the organization does well in its market and the kind of culture it has. Culture directly affects performance: one study of over 200 US firms, all Fortune 500 companies, showed a direct correlation between the nature of the culture and the organization's success, as measured in realities such as share price and net profit.

Culture and beliefs

Essentially, organization culture is about beliefs. It is what people *believe to be true about how things are in the organization*, especially in relation to what is rewarded and what is punished. What we believe to be true will strongly influence how we behave. As an example, here are some commonly held beliefs that we found in one organization that we worked with on transforming its culture:

Belief	Likely impact on behaviour
You have to be male to get to Executive Team level here	Talented women feel angry; fail to apply for promotion; leave
Promotion depends on time-serving	Junior and younger people do not apply for jobs that involve leapfrogging a grade
Verbal articulacy is what matters	People do not necessarily believe senior management pronouncements, seeing them as PR exercises
Intellectual cleverness matters more than generating new business	Failure to generate income; declining fortunes for organization
You have to be an Oxbridge graduate to be taken seriously	Non-Oxbridge graduates feel discouraged; don't apply for the most senior jobs; organization seen as elitist
Your ability to influence events depends on your grade	Communication problems; decision-making getting funnelled upwards; junior people feeling disaffected
Deadlines are not serious	Deadlines are rarely met
There's always a deep pocket somewhere	Cost controls are ineffective
You can't ever sack people for poor performance	People rarely get sacked; it is possible for poor performers to hide in the organization for many years
People can't be confronted about their behaviour	Conflict remains hidden
This is a civilized place to work	It is a civilized place to work; people are polite
The organization looks after its staff	Long-term loyalty to organization; people trade money for security

Why does culture stick?

We have known many chief executives and other senior managers who have come into their jobs with the specific goal of changing the culture. Usually, this has been to transform it from a complacent, slow, bureaucratic organization into one that rewards energy, prudent risk-taking, and customer focus. Less frequently, such chief executives have inherited an unpleasantly thrusting, bullying culture and announced an intention to change to something commercially successful but also more emotionally intelligent. Most such leaders have found it far harder than they had hoped. You do not uproot deeply held beliefs quickly. On many occasions, we have been assured by more junior managers in such organizations, not all of them as cynical as this may seem, that 'These senior managers come and go, they never stay long, and we just get on with our work – we'll be here long after they've left'. In the BBC of the early 1990s, there was a common joke about its notably unpopular Director-General, John Birt (now Lord Birt). This was: 'John believes he is running the BBC, but he is actually running the Virtual BBC, while the Real BBC carries on as normal'. Since so many of this Director-General's innovations were instantly overturned by his successor, Greg Dyke, perhaps there was some truth in this. Typically, it will take anything from three to six years to make a real transformation.

Among the many reasons for the long-lasting nature of beliefs about organization culture are the following: the influence of a powerful founder; solutions that seem to work in the early days of an organization appear to have magical powers so they get perpetuated; the people who fit the culture get rewarded; newcomers are explicitly taught the principles of the culture as part of their induction. A culture may be a benefit or a disadvantage so a 'strong' culture – that is, one that is easily recognized, understood, and acted on – may be a plus or a minus, depending on the beliefs people hold and the behaviour they display as a result.

A non-coaching culture

A non-coaching culture can be easily and unintentionally created, especially when people have lost the links between their personal experience at work, the roles they occupy, the organization's primary business task, and its external environment. These links are essential in creating a culture of engagement – and to a culture where innovation, personal responsibility, and the willingness to tolerate some failure are vital components of business success. Instead, in a non-coaching culture, people can become preoccupied with the internal environment, its rules and regulations, their personal experience, and the personal experience of their colleagues. Faced with the need for change, usually because pressure from the external environment becomes overwhelming, this kind of behaviour can be a real barrier to survival.

One odd feature of organizational culture is how quickly we become used to it. Soon, we stop noticing all those peculiar things that struck us with such force when we were newcomers. It is common to assume that every organization is just like the one we work in, and it can be a huge shock when an organization's senior managers realize how far the organization has got itself unhelpfully stuck. Often this will be because commercial failure reveals that, for instance, an unwieldy hierarchy has destroyed initiative and commitment or that the most senior team are unhealthily disconnected from the people who interact with customers. Sometimes it is an event, trivial in itself, that alerts a boss to the need for significant change. Here is Paul Bates, Deputy Fire Chief for Mid Wales and West Fire and Rescue Services, describing just such an incident:

221

Our wake-up call, about the lack of decision-making in the organization and the perceived need to refer upwards, came when I received a written requisition form to purchase thirty Mars Bars for a sea rescue exercise. Rather than the officer in charge going out and buying the Mars Bars, this straightforward (and potentially life-saving) decision was pushed up the ranks until it landed on my desk. The automatic assumption that permission was needed for such a trivial purchase highlighted that changes were needed. The steps taken to change the culture are beginning to show dividends. Over 100 managers and the senior management team have been trained to use a coaching style of management and this, in turn, has led to improved empowerment, engagement, and appropriate decision-making across the entire organization.

Try this quick quiz to see how far your own organization shows any of the symptoms of a non-coaching culture:

Typical behaviour	Yes ✓	No ✗
There is a pervasive fear of taking risks and being blamed		
Difficult decisions are routinely referred to someone more senior		
Lack of success, either personal or organizational, is typically described in terms of what *others* have done to prevent it		
Staff feel vulnerable, unable to think or act without reference to a rule or protocol		

The tendency is to look inwards to the organization for benchmarks of success rather than to what customers judge to be successful		
Telling and directing is the predominant management style		
Changes are introduced abruptly		
It is difficult for customers/users to make their voices heard		
Feedback is generally restricted to the once-a-year appraisal discussion		
People are unable or unwilling to challenge each other directly		
There are severe restrictions on the learning and development budget		
Staff express private contempt for senior colleagues while appearing respectful to them in public		
'Heroic' figures from the organization's past are idolized		
Staff leak unflattering stories to the media; post critical blogs or Facebook/Twitter comments		

A coaching culture

The opposite of a non-coaching culture is an empowered culture where coaching permeates every interaction whether with staff, suppliers or customers. In a coaching culture, people behave differently:

● They take personal responsibility for their actions: they typically say 'I did so and so', including admitting to mistakes.

223

- People don't get punished for mistakes, especially 'mistakes' that are generated by innovation, unless such mistakes are repeatedly perpetrated and are clearly gross misdemeanours.
- People speak up, even if they have something critical of 'authority' to say.
- Staff seek out responsibility; they look for tasks that will stretch them.
- Coaching becomes the default leadership style for the whole organization.
- Decisions are driven down to the lowest possible level; even the most junior people are encouraged to use their own judgement, especially when dealing with customers.
- Staff automatically expect and get developmental coaching from their immediate bosses.
- Staff use a coaching approach with customers and suppliers.
- Coaching is the basis of the HR and performance management systems.
- There is loyalty to the organization; this includes defending it in public if others attack it.

Essentially, a coaching culture is one where coaching is the predominant style of managing and working together. *Asking* rather than *telling* is the norm and the commitment to improving the organization is embedded in a parallel commitment to improving the people. Coaching becomes not a *technique* to be switched on for special circumstances, such as tackling performance problems in individuals, but is the way a wide range of issues is tackled – for instance, strategic planning and teamwork. Conflict is tackled constructively and early; it becomes natural to take time to help others learn and develop, no matter how important or busy you may be.

Steps to a coaching culture

This is a big subject and we can only touch on the main points here. A comprehensive account of the main issues is the focus of *Managing Coaching at Work* by Jackie Keddy and Clive Johnson (2011). There is also a step-by-step analysis in Peter Hawkins' book, *Creating a Coaching Culture* (2012). Here, we borrow and adapt some ideas from the framework he describes.

The link with the organization's strategy

First, the intention to establish a coaching culture has to be deeply embedded into the strategy for the whole organization. This is easy to write but hard to do. What we observe is that a few heroic early adopters in the organization learn about coaching and become enthusiasts. They are far-sighted, have benefitted from it personally, and become evangelical about what it can do. Typically, such people are not in the most senior ranks – often they are Learning & Development professionals who lack clout at the upper reaches of the organization. Despite this, the organization begins to employ external coaches for some of its most senior people. Because it works, the idea spreads but there is no coherence about who gets coaching or who supplies it, still less any link to what the whole organization needs to do to thrive as a business.

A variant is that the HR department believes that a coaching culture is a jolly good thing, but the aspiration remains an HR initiative. This guarantees that it will fail. HR itself is often seen resentfully as a group of police-like persons who make you do things you otherwise would not wish to do and who are ignorantly or innocently detached from the gritty processes of whatever the core business of the organization is. Even where they have the confidence of the executive team, they may fail to convince colleagues that HR is the means through which the organization's strategy and organization development plan gets delivered, not just an optional add-on.

The questions about strategy and a coaching culture are:

- What is the gap between our stated strategy and where we are currently?
- How do we want coaching to help us close that gap?
- What will a coaching programme cost?
- What kind of return on investment will we get?

To make coaching part of the overall strategy, it is necessary to start with a clear look at what the current culture is and the executive team willing to take responsibility for the ways in which that culture is less than a perfect fit with a coaching culture. This is tough. Many executive teams would rather blame middle managers for their inexplicable refusal to take responsibility than accepting that the behaviour of the executive team is where it all starts. You then need a coaching champion: someone, ideally the CEO, who can explain what coaching is, can talk enthusiastically about its benefits from personal experience, and who is willing to devote a dedicated budget to a programme of culture change in which coaching is the centrepiece.

Managing a cohort of external coaches

Over the last two decades, senior people have discovered that the targeted, time-effective route of coaching creates fast-track learning rather than just relying on standard courses. In some organizations, having a coach used to be a shameful secret, associated with being a poor performer on the brink of being sacked. But that seems like a long time ago. Today, it can be a sign that you have arrived: 'I'm senior enough to have an executive coach now!' beamed one client, proudly reporting his promotion. But executive coaching is expensive. As it grows in popularity, the organization can be dismayed to find that spending on coaching is out of control. The choice of coach is often based on whim and the costs can be hidden in all sorts of unaccountable ways. Where there is no centralized guidance, staff might hire their own coach based on personal recommendation from a colleague, bring a coach with them when they change jobs, or hire an acquaintance who once did a day's 'introduction to coaching' course. The costs can disappear: for instance, we know of people who have paid for their coach out of an expense account, and others who established a so-called Slush Fund from an under-spend, to be explicitly used for coaching. Just as managers used to pass their 'difficult' staff to HR to have the conversations they were too embarrassed or fearful to have themselves, so HR can push the same staff in the direction of an external coach. In this case, the coach is being used inappropriately as a substitute for the performance management that the line manager should be doing. At one coaching conference, the then head of coaching at the retailer, Tesco, revealed her horror at finding that over a million pounds was being spent annually on coaching, but that no one knew who these coaches were, what their quality was or how effective their interventions were. In a global pharmaceutical organization, the incoming Director of HR discovered that it had over seventy different coaches plying their trade in the UK alone. This is not at all unusual.

As part of a commitment to a coaching culture, the organization needs to grip this. When it works well, this is what happens, as it does in organizations like the BBC or the Foreign and Commonwealth Office.

● One person or department becomes a respected source of advice and expertise on coaching. They will develop a policy for coaching and this policy will link with the organization's overall strategy. As part of this strategy, they will define who will benefit from coaching, linking it with the competencies that the organization knows it needs for it to thrive. This person or department may or may not be the budget holder.

- Coaches compete to become accredited suppliers. The organization will set out minimum levels of experience and qualifications and will have a competency framework. There will then be some kind of assessment process where claims to be a brilliant coach are measured against activity that shows the coach in action.

- Costs are rationalized: there will be a sliding scale to reflect different levels of experience and seniority.

- Careful thought is given to matching coaches with clients. Potential clients are encouraged to consider at least two possible coaches and to talk to each before making their final choice.

- The coachee's line manager is routinely involved in a three-cornered meeting involving coach and coachee to agree the agenda for the coaching programme and will connect again to review its success when it ends.

- The organization collects feedback on each coach.

- The coaches are invited to regular meetings to be updated on the organization's needs and for feedback on themes raised by their coaches.

- A measure to assess return on investment is part of the evaluation process.

External coaches need to be treated respectfully as valued suppliers. The best of them will be in demand and may decide that they prefer working for other employers if they dislike the way you deal with them.

Creating an internal cohort of coaches

It does not take long for coaching to become a popular way to develop staff, but few organizations can afford an external coach for everybody who asks for one. Normally it is only the most senior people who qualify. But coaching is too useful to be limited to the upper ranks. This is why so many organizations are training their own cohorts of internal coaches. So, for instance, at the London Deanery, the postgraduate medical school of London University, more than 400 senior doctors have been trained as coaches to other doctors. Over fifty of them have undertaken professional qualifications in coaching and the programme has now spread to the broader question of using coaching with patients in a programme called Coaching for Health.

Depending on the size of the organization, there can be as many as eighty people in an internal cohort of coaches at any one time. These employees will have day jobs and volunteer their time as coaches across the organization, or there may be a much smaller group of full-time coaches. Such people may offer coaching to specific target populations, normally at middle levels, including those:

- making their first transition to a leadership role
- selected to be in a 'talent pool' and needing fast-track development
- being made redundant
- nearing retirement
- changing from a functional to a corporate role
- following up from a leadership development course.

Jackie Keddy is a trainer, writer, coach, and mediator who formerly worked in the Metropolitan Police where she pioneered executive coaching. She describes the results of her pilot project, including the pleasure of seeing that some of the most positive consequences were the unexpected ones of subtly challenging what had traditionally been an intensely hierarchical organization culture:

> We initially trained a cohort of 12 coaches. These were people from all ranks and also included civilian staff. This was the first time that police officers and civilians had been trained together, so it was revolutionary in itself. Senior managers were keen to see what coaching could do for some of the poorer-performing Boroughs in the Met even though I would have felt happier had we chosen less problematical Boroughs. The coaches were typically coaching people more senior than themselves – for instance, I was a Detective Chief Inspector at the time but one of my coachees was a Commander – i.e. three grades higher than me. We found that the coachees were unconcerned by grade differences as long as they were reassured that the coach was trained. Altogether, the project was very successful: anecdotally we had evidence that sickness absence rates and grievance levels fell. People felt more empowered and listened to; morale and team motivation improved. The coaches found that giving time and some simple affirmation went a long way with our clients and that success did not depend in any way on the coach being of a similar rank to the client.

To counter suspicions that this is coaching-lite and a feeble substitute for the supposed glamour and expertise of an external coach, the organization needs to invest in serious selection, training, and accreditation of those who come forward. Such coaches will need feedback from their clients, professional supervision, and updating. Those who prove unsatisfactory have to be weeded out and at the same time you need to be constantly recruiting newcomers to replace those who leave. Research by the Institute of Leadership and Management (ILM) in 2011 reported some interesting findings. Of the 250 organizations surveyed, 80 per cent had used or were actually using coaching as a development tool, mostly to middle and more senior managers. There was broad consensus about the value of coaching. However, the report also commented:

> **More support is required for internal coaches:** Coaching is a discipline, a complex practical skillset that requires hands-on experience, evaluation and refinement. A greater focus on developing internal coaching capacity is needed. Most organisations recognise the value of coaching qualifications. Two-thirds (66%) offer development options for coaches such as in-house training (20%), management development programmes (11%) or one-to-one train-the-trainer support (8%).

> One third (34%), however, do not offer any support or development for internal coaches.

Our own, admittedly anecdotal, experience is that investing in properly accredited training for internal coaches remains rare.

However, investing in a programme of the type offered by the ILM has many benefits because it provides a rigorous academic and practical framework for developing coaching skills. The people who train and work as internal coaches report becoming better leaders themselves, of having greater awareness of what is happening across the organization, and acquiring a set of wonderfully useful life skills. For instance, using internal coaches has helped the Welsh Government develop the management and leadership skills across the Welsh public sector for a fraction of the cost of other development initiatives. Over 250 middle and senior managers across the public sector in Wales have been trained as coaches and have achieved or are working towards an ILM coaching qualification. To raise the standard and quality of internal coaches (and overcome the misconception that internal coaching is cheap and cheerful but not very good), Public Service Management Wales (PSMW), the leadership and development arm of the Welsh Government, established a coaching collaborative and peer supervision sessions to help the internal coaches share best practice and develop their skills further.

Dr. Neil Wooding, Director of PSMW, explains:

> This initiative has raised the awareness of what internal coaching offers in terms of helping leaders, their teams and organizations achieve more with less resource. We are delighted with the buy-in and support we have achieved. Over 50 Senior Executives have now been trained to use coaching and develop a coaching culture within their organizations – which has helped to make this initiative such a success.

Coaching as the default leadership and management style

The ILM research emphasized how far we have to go before coaching becomes more than a privilege associated with the talent pipeline, let alone becoming the default management style of the organization. Again, this will not happen by accident. In fact, the only chance it has of becoming real is if real budget and real expertise are devoted to it. This means clarifying how coaching as a general skill, applied by someone who is not your line manager, is different from coaching someone who reports to you. Of course, this is the very topic of this book, but reading a book is a poor substitute for actual training with practice, rigorous feedback, and guidance.

Such training will only work if it starts with the executive team, including the CEO, is steadily introduced through the same training to every manager at every level in the organization, and then embedded in the organization's HR processes, especially its recruitment and appraisal systems. It makes no sense whatsoever to say you aspire to a coaching culture and then to go on retaining or promoting people who show no sign of being able to change from dysfunctional styles of management. Nor does it make sense to recruit people without the temperament and aptitude to learn how to coach. One sign that you are on your way to a coaching culture would be to see whether coaching skills have become one of the core competencies for which the organization assesses at selection stage. If this is not the case, then the organization is unlikely to be serious about creating a coaching culture.

The benefits of developing coaching as the default leadership and management style are multi-layered. For instance, managers themselves become far less stressed, as vividly described by Ailsa McBean, Integrated Service Manager at Monmouthshire County Council:

I was so impressed with the 2 day 'Manager as Coach' programme that I decided to implement what I'd learnt immediately. Realizing that instead of helping my staff by 'telling' them what to do, I was in fact making them dependent on me and stopping them from coming to their solutions was a light bulb moment for me. I put my coaching skills and OSCAR into practice immediately. I rolled out the training to my team of social workers, all of whom were under huge pressure and completely stressed, turning to me for guidance, help and support on a daily basis. They in turn started to use a coaching style with their clients.

I remember feeling guilty as I now literally had hours of free time, and it hit me how much of my time had been spent 'rescuing' my staff, doing their work for them (all the time thinking I was being a kind, supportive manager). After just a few months the difference in my team was palpable, stress was reduced, absenteeism was down, confidence was high and instead of going home drained I now had time on my hands.

As a result of all this free time I was able to focus on my own career development and within six months was promoted twice – all of this due to coaching rather than telling!

And as we described in Chapter 2, coaching as the default management style is closely linked with creating staff engagement, itself closely correlated with business success.

Coaching customers, suppliers, and service users

When you stand apprehensively at the British Airways self check-in, the member of the airline's staff who is hovering nearby is available to coach you through the process if it is the first time you are using it, and so is that pleasant member of the Sainsbury's team who will show you how to scan your own shopping in the hope that next time you will be able to do it on your own. When your GP offers two or three choices of treatment, backed up by carefully phrased information, he or she is using a coaching approach: you are the one who will live with the results of your treatment, not the doctor.

You may need to buy an insurance policy for your pet and when the call centre staffer replies, you may find that far from deluging you with facts that you cannot take in, or trying to bludgeon you into a sale, you are actually being coached through which of the many options would suit you best, even if it is the cheapest of those available and therefore apparently less profitable for the seller.

Computer technology has revolutionized the way services are provided. Within living memory, to take just a few examples, petrol stations had people who came onto the forecourt to serve you and sometimes expected to be tipped; the office photocopier had to be serviced by an expert; you bought your groceries from a small shop where the owner picked your chosen goods off the shelves and personally wrapped them in brown paper and string; you paid your energy bills by taking cash to the electricity or gas showroom; you made a trip to the theatre box office and queued to buy tickets; you booked your holiday travel through visiting a high street travel agent.

Today we customers can do all of this for ourselves and many companies have moved from providing the service into coaching their customers. All of this is associated with commercial success. Wise companies know that if you think of creating wealth simply for shareholders, you may achieve short-term success while also potentially creating longer-term problems, whereas if you think of providing benefit for all your stakeholders (e.g. staff, suppliers, customers), sustainable success is much more likely. The twentieth-century approach was a so-called 'value chain': how processes add financial value to raw ingredients. So a humble potato bought by the manufacturer for fractions of pence becomes potato crisps through a range of processes that means it can be sold for hundreds of percent more. The twentieth-first-century approach is to see a different kind of value chain running along in parallel – an *affiliative value chain*: one where the value added is about the quality of the relationships and long-term brand loyalty. We are reminded here of Jan Carlzon, the former Chief Executive of SAS. SAS had been notorious as the worst airline in Europe and was a heavily loss-making enterprise. In the early 1980s, Carlzon stood with a stopwatch discreetly observing his airline's customers, discovering that what he called *moments of truth* were typically only a few seconds long. These were the fleeting moments where the customer interacted with staff, for instance, booking, checking in, asking for information, being served food, retrieving baggage. The quality of these personal exchanges was what decided the customer's view of the airline and influenced their future buying decisions. This was true then and it is still true now. Carlzon's *Putting People First* programme gave front line staff the then revolutionary authority to sort out a customer's problems instantly rather than having to ask permission from a manager. Within a short time, SAS was highly profitable and had become the beacon for all other airlines.

This approach to customers is only possible in an organization in which staff are well treated by their bosses and are on the receiving end of coaching themselves. A sure sign that this is not the case is any organization in which staff combine surliness or indifference with an inflexible rules-is-rules attitude to customers. If your boss treats you like a naughty child, is rude or fails to consult you, then for certain this is the behaviour you will faithfully reproduce with customers. Whereas if you know your boss is keenly interested in your development, nourishes the relationship with you, and you are getting coaching from him or her as a matter of routine, then this is what you will feel motivated to do with customers.

Using coaching as a sales method

Coaching is a far superior way to sell goods and services than the old approaches that too often badgered the customer with product knowledge they did not need and used bullying tactics to make a sale. When on the receiving end of this kind of selling, you feel hunted and your instinct is to do what any hunted animal does – get away as quickly as possible. The coaching approach is based on creating rapport with the customer by first of all establishing their needs, assessing their present situation, and then moving on to options. Selling with integrity means that you never sell a customer something that does not suit their needs, however tempting it might seem. This is the principled approach to selling. Although it has not explicitly been described as 'coaching', the Huthwaite sales training company's approach, *'SPIN'* selling developed by Neil Rackham (1988), and Sharon Drew Morgen's (1997) *Buying Facilitation* methods are in fact closely allied to coaching. Companies using such approaches will normally greatly increase their sales because their approach to selling is underpinned by integrity and is aimed at meeting buyers' needs. Neither buyers nor sales-people feel under pressure. OSCAR works here too:

Accompanying a friend about to get married and on a wedding-buying trip to Milan, one of us enjoyed seeing this approach in action at the fashion retailer Max Mara. First, the customer was warmly greeted by an individual who introduced herself by name and said she was available if we wanted her. Yes, we did. She asked what help we needed. The bride, a well-informed customer with a keen sense of what suited her, reeled off a list of potential items for which she had saved hard. This was the O of OSCAR. There then followed a brief conversation about what she already had (S: Situation), identifying where the gaps were in her wardrobe and what her criteria were for making choices, for instance neutral colours, cost, classic styles. At the C (Choices and Consequences) phase, we sat in a well-lit, comfortable cubicle while our sales assistant-coach roamed the shop. Various pieces were then tried, discarded, tried again – maybe with a different belt or shoes. The assistant offered frank but tactful feedback and made a number of good suggestions, all of this helpful, relaxed, and the opposite of the over-pushy sales approach that can be so intimidating. The Action and Review phases were about calculating the costs, making last-minute changes, and then reviewing how well the pieces worked together and had met her original criteria. As a transaction, this was wholly successful for both sides. The sales assistant must have enjoyed doing an excellent job for the customer as well as making a substantial sale for her employer. The customer felt highly satisfied with her purchases, not least because of the friendly and respectful way that she had been treated as a sensible partner in the process, and in fact several years on, everything she bought is still being worn with pleasure and she is still a loyal Max Mara customer.

Coaching is also transforming the way sales staff relate to customers. The essence of the approach is that customers are treated as partners fully able to make up their own minds about what they buy. The aim is long-term loyalty based on demonstrating that you understand and are interested in what the customer needs, rather than being frantic to make a sale, whatever the consequences. You can see this most clearly in cold calling. Whereas cold calling using a stilted, scripted approach has a notably low success rate, the coaching approach has a high success rate, so the bottom-line impact is substantial.

The OSCAR framework works well as a selling tool. It emphasizes building rapport and thoroughly exploring the customer's needs and only then moving into the selling phase.

Using OSCAR in a sales situation

OUTCOME Questions to ask yourself in advance	• What is your long-term outcome with this customer? • What is the customer trying to achieve? • What would success look like for your customer? • What would you like to achieve from the sales call? *Task: preparing yourself for the call*
SITUATION Questions to ask the customer	• What is the current situation? • What problems are you facing? • How are you currently addressing those challenges? • What are your most pressing needs? *Task: building rapport; showing that you understand the customer*
CHOICES AND CONSEQUENCES Describing your offer, its features and benefits; encouraging the customer to articulate their choices	• What choices do you have? • What options are you considering? • May I describe what we offer? (Set out features and benefits) • How far does this seem to meet what you need? • What are your choices here? • What are the consequences of each choice? • Which choices have the best consequences?

	Task: setting out your product 'offer'; anticipating and handling objections; emphasizing the customer's choices; being prepared to walk away if what you offer and what the customer needs are not well matched; showing that you are helping the customer to explore all options
ACTIONS	• Where do we go from here? • How do you feel about taking the next steps? • What else do you need from me? Task: gaining commitment from the customer to act on what you have agreed
REVIEW	• How will the decision be made? • Who else will be involved in making the decision? • When could I contact you again? • How do we review progress? Task: understanding the decision-making process and keeping yourself in the loop; shortening the sales cycle

Coaching service users

It may not be immediately obvious how coaching could work with service users, such as the clients of social services departments – whether carers or recipients of services. Especially where services are free at the point of delivery, service users tend to feel grateful for whatever they receive and the power is most definitely in the hands of the service provider. Furthermore, some of the clients of such services are among the most vulnerable in society: those living with chronic disability, the elderly and poor. But many professionals are now discovering the power of coaching. When doctors and nurses use it with patients, they can be astonished at the results achieved. A report in a respected medical journal in 2009 commented that 'patients and not healthcare providers are the primary managers of their conditions'. It is too soon for overall research results on the many projects now working in this area, but early data from Medica, a health insurer in the USA, showed that people who took up the offer of having a fully trained 'health coach' had massively increased quality-of-life scores, their numbers of hospital admissions fell, and their cholesterol results improved. Another similar programme showed that teenage patients with diabetes, a group notoriously reluctant to comply with their prescribed treatments, were much more likely to commit to their medication when they had had sessions with practice nurses trained as coaches. The overall impact on the health budget could be worth many billions of pounds, for instance, reducing unnecessary prescribing and preventing emergency and acute-care admissions. A report in 2010 from the School of Pharmacy at the University of London found that some £300 million annually was wasted on unused or unfinished prescriptions and that was for England alone.

The difference is that working in genuine partnership with patients, especially those with long-term chronic conditions, encourages them to take responsibility for their own health and to make informed choices. Differences in clinician behaviour can look small and subtle but actually they come from a transformed attitude to the patient. The clinicians quoted below, trained as coaches through the London Deanery programme (p. 229), soon realized that what worked with colleagues would also work with patients.

> I thought I already did treat patients as partners, but I realize now that I didn't. The main change has been in my attitude: I assume that they are perfectly capable of taking a resourceful approach to their own health, especially where lifestyle choices can have a big

impact on prognosis. In effect I help them now to design their own lifestyle programmes and it makes all the difference in the world.

(Cardiac surgeon)

I no longer have 'heartsink' patients, the people who trudge in and out of your surgery week after week and leave you feeling so terribly inadequate as their doctor. Something as simple as agreeing an Outcome for the consultation and doing some close listening and summarizing changes everything. So instead of asking 'What seems to be the problem?' or 'What can I do for you today?', I now say [after a polite greeting] words to the effect of, 'What do you need to get out of this consultation?' The effect is truly amazing. You get to the heart of their worries more or less instantly. I realize now how often I must have been wrong in my assumptions about what patients needed from me.

(General practitioner)

My first trial run with OSCAR was with a patient who was struggling with withdrawal symptoms after giving up smoking. Previously I would probably have jumped straight to telling, advising, and prescribing. It turned out that what he really wanted was ideas on how to get through the first hour after getting up every day, and underneath that, some encouragement to keep going. He already had all the ideas he needed really, but it was very satisfying to use the framework with him, especially the Choices and Consequences part. We zoomed through it with high energy. Eight weeks on and he's still a non-smoker, whereas I think he would probably have started smoking again by now if I'd done my usual thing.

(Nurse-practitioner)

Using coaching with suppliers

Supplier–customer relationships can be fraught. Where the supplier has a premium product or service for which there is high demand, the customer may have to put up with sloppy service bought at a high price. Where the reverse is true, in other words where there is an over-supply of the service or product, the customer may force prices down to the point where the supplier goes out of business. Mutual bad temper and resentment can often characterize these transactions. Here, too, coaching and the OSCAR framework can help, with the lead being taken by either side. Where an organization is committed to a coaching culture, coaching can seep into these conversations too. The following account by a sales director shows how powerful it can be, even where you feel you are starting at a disadvantage:

We make a particular product, simple but essential, and we sell to the NHS among other customer groups, but the product has become more or less commoditized and we have many competitors. I accept that the NHS is under an obligation to get the best possible deal they can. The trouble is that we are a relatively small firm and were already making a pretty narrow margin on this product. The guy doing the procurement for a major NHS buyer contacted me with a rather cold-sounding email to say that unless we reduced our prices they would buy elsewhere. I knew they could, even though I believe the quality we offer has the edge against competitors and that is important in this field. Because I'd had the coaching training I thought I'd give it a try. I arranged a phone call with him and knew it was the relationship that would swing it, if anything could. I stated my outcome (the O), which was to establish what needed to happen for us to keep the contract, emphasizing that we had always enjoyed the relationship with them and felt proud of supplying the NHS. He agreed to this readily enough while warning me of the intense pressure to contain costs. We then went to Situation and I asked him to tell me about the demands he was under. This probably took about ten minutes with me doing a lot of rapport-building through listening and summarizing. I did no pushing or 'selling' at this stage. What emerged was exactly who he needed to satisfy and how – and it was clear there was some room for manoeuvre as he said the clinical teams really like our product and there is feedback that they actually prefer it to that of the rivals. When we got to Choices and Consequences, I asked if we could just play with a few ideas without committing to any of them. He agreed. The best option emerged from this discussion, which was that we would maintain the price on our premium product but reduce the price on the standard one in return for a slightly bigger order and a reduction in the fulfilment time and delivery cost. He was pleased with this, as it allowed him to satisfy the money people and also keep the clinicians on board. We discussed how we could re-contact their lead people to get ideas about clinical needs just emerging. That way we can gain the edge over competitors by being ready with new product, including using them as a pilot group. The Action was to confirm this in writing and the Review stage was an agreement to talk again in a few months. The margin is still slim but we have kept the client – and in a recession that's what matters, so thank you OSCAR!

Coaching here is a close cousin to negotiation and mediation, both of which use similar skills.

Return on investment

There has to be a bottom line benefit to all of this, so how do you calculate it? *With some difficulty* is the answer. Evaluation is tricky. To do it properly you need to have a benchmark at the outset – perhaps a staff survey, an employee engagement survey or a comprehensive set of 360-degree feedback evaluations for a large population of managers. Then, ideally, you need to have a control group – a set of managers who have not been exposed to training in how to coach and an experimental group who have been so exposed. Over a period of, say, a year, you would then compare how the control group's performance against your original benchmarks compared with those of the experimental group. This would give you some idea of what behaviour shifts, if any, your experimental group had made. But this still would not tell you how the organization had benefited in bottom line terms. To do that you would probably have to be patient enough to measure change over at least a two-year period, and to have some reliable metrics to correlate the manager's behaviour change with improvements in measurable performance – for instance, increases in turnover, reductions in costs, staff retention, reductions in cycle time and re-work, profit margin.

Most organizations do not do this. They embark on an enthusiastic road to creating a coaching culture without any baseline. Not least, running evaluative surveys costs time and money and you have to be certain that the costs justify the data you obtain. This is why so much of the evidence is anecdotal.

Evaluation is a more complex question than it may seem. You may want to distinguish between the investment in coach training and the eventual investment in coaching itself. You can ask people whether they have enjoyed the training they receive, but people can enjoy training without necessarily benefiting from it and they may sometimes hate the training but be able to learn from it. If what people learn on training courses is not supported by the entire culture in the organization, the lessons of the training fade and the skills decay. Not least, some of the most important factors are intangible, for instance, happiness at work, fit with personal values and skills, how hard people are willing to work.

When employing external coaches, it is vital to collect feedback from coachees. Patterns may or may not emerge around particular coaches, and in any case, such evidence is anecdotal – it only tells you what the coachee has felt about the coach, not whether the coaching has been effective. Some studies place too much emphasis on the results of an unconvincingly small sample or on one particular way of capturing data. Some fail to remember that differences in departmental or national culture can introduce complications. Departments or individuals who come forward for coaching may already be different – perhaps more forward looking – from those who do not. Changes in human behaviour can rarely be attributed to a single cause and where coaching has appeared to work – or to fail – there will be many other factors that have contributed. In general, it is safer to take a 'balance of probabilities' approach, similar to that used in civil law (rather than criminal law, where absolute proof is the aim) where all the evidence appears to point in the same direction.

Some simple ways of calculating return on investment in coaching training

- Administer an employee engagement staff survey that will allow you to see results by department and manager.

- Develop a brief 360-feedback questionnaire for every manager, remembering to include feedback for everyone who takes part.
- Deliver the coaching training.
- Administer both surveys again, once more offering feedback.
- Calculate the differences.
- Ask participants in the coach training plus their bosses and direct reports what tangible effects in bottom line terms (impact on clients and customers) they have observed.

Two case studies

Here is how RS Components has seen changes resulting from their investment in coaching training. The Group distributes 550,000 products worldwide, ranging from semiconductors and optoelectronics to power tools and protective clothing. Their productivity and performance have been outstanding and in fact revenues, profits, and share price have consistently improved, despite the recession. Sara Wright, their Head of Leadership and Organization Development, spearheaded a Leadership Coaching Programme that has been in place since 2008, and during this time over 300 leaders and managers have completed a four-month, in-depth, rigorous programme to train them in coaching. Sara recognizes that with so many variables it is tricky to make hard and fast claims for a single intervention such as training in coaching, but they are tracking changes through feedback from staff and linking this with results on employee engagement.

> The programme exceeded our expectations, as the impact on individuals was tremendous. Qualitative feedback from delegates indicated that their confidence

increased; many experienced a shift in mindset as well as behaviour. Over twenty senior managers who completed the externally accredited programme are now coaching supervisors on the internal programme. This supports the cascade approach and embeds the learning.

Quantitative evidence from the 180-degree feedback scores taken at the end of the programme indicates that employees are noticing a positive change in their line managers. This 180 questionnaire on skills, capabilities, and beliefs tells us that our managers are consistently scoring above 7 on a 1 to 10 scale. The questionnaire also measures perceived business benefit, with the average from the question 'My coaching has directly resulted in business benefits' scoring 7.04.

The Executive Committee has set challenging and yet realistic targets for the employee engagement survey. The survey includes a number of questions that specifically ask about the mindset and behaviour shift in our management population and the results rely on a coaching and 'adult' culture. We are actively changing the culture by seeking to change the mindset of our managers from a basis of expert power where they always know the answer, to one where managers believe others have the potential to grow. We describe this as an 'adult' culture rather than the well-meaning but paternalistic culture it is replacing.

It is noticeable that there is reduced task-related micro decision-making at the top as senior leaders focus on more strategic decisions and delegate task-related decisions; this is reflected in the Executive Committee agenda. The pace of change has improved dramatically.

> Recent re-structures and redundancy programmes have been implemented smoothly and have treated people with dignity. This has helped the cultural shift as the 'adult' culture starts to take effect in our communications, employee development interventions, and reward programmes. People are starting to take ownership of their careers and leaders have coaching conversations rather than being directive about careers.

IAG New Zealand is part of the wider Insurance Australia Group, a general insurance business with leading brands across its home markets of Australia and New Zealand, a growing presence in Asia, and other specialist underwriting operations. In 2008, the New Zealand business was faced with some challenges across their business results and staff engagement scores. These were warning signs that could not be ignored. The implementation of coaching programmes was aimed at addressing these issues and was advocated by the CEO at a strategic level to support a wider cultural change.

IAG New Zealand invested in coach training for its managers with an internal framework to support continued coaching development. An unexpected outcome was that some managers adapted the coaching framework, a little like OSCAR, into a sales methodology that places the emphasis on creating rapport with customers by enquiry into customers' needs. Jake Harding, Senior HR manager, takes up the story:

> We needed to change the culture of the organization and introducing coaching for managers was one crucial part of the strategy for doing this. The aim was to improve business results by addressing the way

managers had conversations with their people, working with them to focus more keenly on business outcomes and helping them face the changes ahead. We developed two programmes, one a short introduction to coaching that is mandatory for all managers, the other we called Coach-Leader, a three-month 'master coach' accreditation for people who show an aptitude for coaching. These master coaches then coach internal coachees for a six-month assignment.

We soon saw how radically effective this could be. For instance, when Malia Apikotoa stepped into her new role as State Northern Sales Manager in mid-2011, she was enrolled on to the Coach-Leader programme as a coachee. She made coaching a priority with her Team Leaders and within their teams. The combination has had a powerful positive impact in every way: her staff are reporting to be more engaged and their results have improved in the short time Malia has used this approach.

Malia attibutes this turnaround to the confidence she gained to apply the methods learned in her coach training and when she herself was coached. She has learnt the power of open questions and of exploring options and generating alternative ways of thinking that improve their own performance.

She says: 'For example, I want my staff to write 500 items next month. But I don't say "I want you to write 500 items next month!" Instead, we put their results on the table and I ask thinking questions such as: How would it feel if you increased it? What obstacles do you think there are? How would you feel if you had written 500? What kind of incentive can we put in place to ensure this is a great goal for you and one worth celebrating?'

Furthermore, we do this using simple language by developing the ability to be succinct, specific, and generous. This is critical because all coaching sessions are timely, effective, and efficient, which is proven by their results – these results can easily be adapted into their personal lives as well because we value work–life balance. A happy staff member is an achieving staff member.

Business impact – Malia's results

Malia's results showed immediate improvement:

	% of team achieving 'solid performance' (i.e. on budget)	New business items, % of target	Referalls, % of target
Quarter 1 start	37.5	86	75
Quarter 1 end	89	96	89
Total business benefit	+NZ$589,000		

For the modest investment IAG made in Mailia's training, this is a truly stunning result over a very short period of time.

Other impressive results

The CEO in Australia of the restaurant chain, Wagamama, Australia, is described by Keddy and Johnson (2011) as attributing their recovery from the brink of disaster to their investment in coaching. Coaching was aimed at general managers and played a key role in facilitated team events. Learning to give and receive non-judgemental feedback helped de-mystify what 'good performance' really meant. Staff turnover fell, 'mystery diner' scores improved significantly, and profitability increased sharply.

Even the simplest and most anecdotal evidence on the benefits of coaching invariably shows all of the following:

- more engaged staff who are more willing to make well-judged decisions that benefit customers
- lowered costs through implementing staff ideas
- briefer meetings
- better quality decision-making
- retention of the most talented staff
- reduced stress all round.

A way of calculating return on investment

One way of calculating return on investment in coaching has been developed by the US consulting firm Sherpa Coaching. This still involves some inspired guesswork, but is as good as any other way of calculating something so slippery and intangible. You start by calculating the cost to the business of failing to resolve some issue. Mostly such costs are hidden, but they are present none the less. So failing to resolve an issue might involve any of the following:

- Increased sickness absence; hiring an occupational health doctor to assess the person.
- Demotivating effect on others.
- Increased chances of mistakes, any of which might incur a cash cost to rectify.
- Hiring temporary staff to cover for absence or incompetence.

- Legal advice on employment law if the person fails to improve.
- Lost revenue as a result of client complaints.
- Money involved in settling compensation claims as a result of avoidable mistakes.
- Costs of service recovery after an avoidable crisis.
- Costs of a compromise agreement if you want a poor performer to leave quietly.
- Recruitment costs to find a replacement: agencies, advertising, bedding-in period while the new person learns the job. Costs of replacement in such circumstances are generally reckoned to be anything from 100 per cent to 250 per cent of the new person's first-year salary.

Here is how the Sherpa protocol works:

Step 1	Estimate the total value of resolving an issue – or the costs involved in *not* resolving it.
	Example: You are a manager who has successfully coached a poor performer, tackling her lack of skills in her job, uncovering hidden skills, and successfully deploying her to another part of the business where she is performing well.
	Avoided redundancy and recruitment costs and disruption to business, added ability to add value to new part of the business.
	Benefit: £80,000
Step 2	Multiply the sum you arrived at in Step 1 by the percentage you attribute to the coaching: let's say this is 50 per cent =
	£40,000 (half of £80,000)
Step 3	How confident are you in the accuracy of Steps 1 and 2?
	Let's say the answer is that you are 80 per cent confident.
	Adjusted total benefit: £32,000 (80% of £40,000)

Step 4	Subtract the cost of coaching: no cash costs – it took about three hours of your time plus the cost of investment in your training as a coach, so giving it a notional cost, maybe £1000 at most. **Net benefit: £31,000 (£32,000 – £1000)**
Step 5	To calculate return on investment, divide the net benefit by the cost of coaching and turn into a percentage. In this case: £31,000/£1000 × 100 = 3100% **Return on investment = 3100%**

As in investment, this is astounding. The results may be even more startling if you apply it to assessing how coaching your staff can develop successful new products and services for the organization. Try it yourself and see what kind of result you get.

Sustaining momentum

There have been many organizational improvement ideas in the recent past: Management by Objectives, Total Quality Management (TQM), Business Process Re-engineering (BPR), Empowerment, Learning Organizations, and so on. All were designed to bring about large-scale improvement and all had their moment – but ultimately failed. What will keep coaching from the same fate? Essentially, it will be enthusiastic high-level sponsorship that links coaching to business results, combined with allocating enough resources to create real momentum over an extended period. This will include devoting generous budgets to training, designing systems that track effectiveness, creating human support that provides continuing opportunities to build skill, constantly promoting success stories, and accepting that some backsliding is inevitable. Unlike innovations such as BPR and TQM, coaching can be done every day in small bites by anyone and does not need elaborate processes of restructuring to make it effective, but it will still need passion, determination, and constant initiatives and support mechanisms to keep impetus going.

Our clients sometimes ask whether it is better to announce some kind of 'Big Bang' intervention for coaching with glitzy presentations and roadshows. These seem to run the risk of being met with cynicism, characterized by change-weary staff as yet another over-ambitious initiative that can probably be safely ignored. Expectations of instant transformation are usually unrealistic given how long it takes an organization culture to change. Our own experience suggests that a cautious approach with an initial and well-assessed pilot project works best. A planned and larger-scale programme involving more people can then follow.

Summary

Developing a coaching culture is a wholehearted approach to the entire way an organization does business. It starts with linking coaching to the overall strategy and having a coaching policy whose function is to be part of how the strategy is delivered. The CEO is directly involved as an enthusiastic sponsor. Coaching will affect every aspect of the culture, including training all managers in how coaching can become the default leadership and management style, playing its part in creating staff engagement and assessment at selection stage, as well as being part of the organization's performance review processes. It will involve the most senior people in having external coaches while simultaneously developing a cohort of internally trained and accredited volunteer coaches who are not in line management relationships with the people they coach. In addition, the coaching philosophy and skills will permeate the relationships with all stake-holders: customers, shareholders, suppliers, and staff. All of this will be based on the assumption that it makes good business sense – with an impressive return on investment and a positive impact on the bottom line.

Even if you have been convinced by our ideas in this book, you may still have understandable niggling doubts – the subject of our final chapter.

10 WHAT'S STOPPING YOU?

When we run courses for line managers on how to incorporate coaching into the way they do their jobs, the most common reactions include: relief that there really is a way forward that does not involve the two extremes of either shouting or half-heartedly ignoring performance problems; an acknowledgement that it is all obvious and the OSCAR framework just elegantly codifies common sense; and sometimes the stoutly made claim that the manager concerned is 'doing it anyway'. We find it hard to remember a single participant who has told us that this is all gobbledegook, or just a fad, or too hard to do. Given that this is the case, why might you still have hesitations about incorporating coaching into your everyday work?

Being a lone voice

One possible reason for hesitating is that you may see yourself as a lone voice, a single person adopting a coaching approach when all around you are behaving in whatever way is traditional in your organization. This is why the material we explored in the previous chapter is so important. Coaching is obviously much easier if it is explicitly endorsed and rewarded as the default way of managing in the entire organization. However, if you believe this approach is the best way to get results, do it! It will be easier if other managers are doing the same, especially if this is the behaviour of the most senior people, but it will get results, even if your own unit is the one bright spot in an otherwise dark place.

When you try out coaching behaviour for the first time, it is normal for it to feel 'clunky' – a word we hear a lot from newly trained managers. 'They'll know I've been on a course and mock me', they cry, or, 'I still can't make it sound natural'.

There is some truth in the 'clunkiness' argument. We introduced the 'change and competence curve' in relation to organizations (p. 207) but it applies just as readily to individuals. At the bottom, with Unconscious Incompetence, you are innocent of how incompetent you are. For instance, many of the people we train start off by believing that they are already using coaching and are shocked to discover that what they have actually been doing is pressing their own ideas on people, though doing it nicely. When you understand your own incompetence you progress to Conscious Incompetence: a daunting stage because now you know how much there is to learn and it feels overwhelming. Bit by bit you begin to put it all together and to feel a little more confident. Then you come to the 'clunkiness' stage: Conscious Competence. This is where you have to think through every action, pause before framing every sentence, it feels difficult and unnatural, and you are sure everyone can see your hesitations and unease. If you think back to when you were learning to drive, this is the phase where you have mastered the various skills such as using the mirrors, or parking, but cannot do it without a great deal of conscious effort and concentration. As with learning to drive, the only way to conquer this feeling is committing to the practice, which will help develop your own unique style. For instance, where coaching is concerned, you will customize the standard questions you have learnt on the course and flex them to your own circumstances. Once you do this, you will eventually pass to the final stage of Unconscious Competence where coaching is not a special 'technique', it simply becomes what you do. You no longer have to think carefully before phrasing your questions or wonder, 'Is this an occasion where coaching would be useful?' Unfortunately, like any skill worth having, it is impossible to leap straight from Unconscious Incompetence to Unconscious Competence. Awareness, feedback, and commitment to practice are what will make the difference.

Psychological barriers

Some of the assumed barriers to coaching are psychological. One of the most familiar is this one: *They don't want responsibility so I can't coach them. They just want to be told what to do.* Again there may be truth in this. People who have never been given responsibility can grow fearful of it. In some organizations there is wholehearted aversion to risk, often on the good grounds that when people have taken risks that have gone awry, they have been punished. It can then feel enormously effortful to go against the grain. However, take heart. We describe in Chapters 1 and 2 the terrible costs of such cultures, costs that have deleterious effects on the bottom line as well as on people's sense of wellbeing, all of which hinges on feeling in control: one of our prime needs as human beings. You can never feel in control if your life is one of being constantly told what to do, even when this is done from benign motives. Actually, coaching is probably the only way to encourage people to take responsibility. And the costs of not doing it are high.

Allied with the assumed helplessness of staff members is the assumption that *Coaching takes too long; I haven't got time for it, it's quicker just to tell.* There are several misconceptions wrapped up in this one. One is the idea that coaching means holding lengthy, tortuous conversations. Occasionally this might be true, but as we hope we have shown, when coaching becomes your default style of managing, a coaching conversation is more likely to be just a few minutes long and the kind of discussion you have frequently and informally rather than as an occasional protracted set-piece. The time involved in a directive style of managing is actually much greater long term. So you tell them – and mysteriously, they forget, so you tell them again and they forget again and by now you are exasperated with their hopelessness so you issue orders but not so pleasantly, and then finally in exasperation, you irritably do whatever it is yourself, at the cost of getting your own proper job done, thus creating the familiar cycle of over-stressed senior managers and lacklustre, unmotivated team members. Which saves more time eventually – investing twenty minutes in a coaching conversation or spending many hours standing over people while they wait for you to tell them what to do?

Occasionally we meet people on our courses who are fearful of giving up what they assume has been their recipe for professional success. They will usually describe a directive style of managing which they characterize as 'firm', 'confident' or 'decisive'. When we carry out confidential feedback surveys for these managers, it is nearly always the case that their colleagues, especially their direct reports, often see 'authoritative' as bossy, 'confident' as egotistical, and 'decisive' as arrogant. While of course it is true that such behaviour can get short-term results, long term it is destructive and professional success has usually been achieved despite such behaviour not because of it.

Another variant of this defence against using coaching is to characterize it as *touchy-feely*, the ultimately despised approach, implying that anyone who is not 'firm/'decisive' – add your own euphemism for 'directive' – is a soft-headed wuss. Abundant research shows the enormously deleterious effects of a directive style but the accusation that coaching is 'soft' is a profound misunderstanding of what it really entails. Coaching involves a different kind of toughness, a kind that is tenacious, 100 per cent committed to getting the highest standards of performance out of people, and one that is respectful of their individuality and potential.

Professional and technical identity

Many people have arrived at a managerial role through mastery of a professional or technical area of expertise. It is striking how difficult it can be to let this go

When I became Medical Director [the most senior doctor in a hospital], I had no idea what was truly required of me. I still saw myself as a doctor not a manager, even though my role is essentially managerial, albeit a medical manager. It was only when my colleagues on the executive team pointed out that I was wearing 'scrubs' to executive team meetings even though I wasn't on call that I realized how wrong I was getting it. It was like an in-your-face statement that I was really a doctor and not one of those 'Suits'. Very naive and silly as I now see.

My early jobs were all as a management accountant. I got promoted to my first role as a manager, leading a team of other accountants. It took me a long time to understand that this wasn't just about being a super-accountant, just a little bit cleverer than them. It was extremely hard to let go of that identity and the expertise that went with it. I kept on wanting to solve their problems for them. Once I'd done the coaching training I saw that my role was to develop them, including developing them so that in terms of their technical expertise they overtook me.

Many managers will recognize these portraits. Promotion to a yet more senior managerial role can come as a shock. It's not usually about doing just what you were doing before but on a bigger scale. It is a different role where delegation is essential, releasing you to do the networking, forward-thinking, and leadership that goes with it. This can create crippling anxiety: How do I do this? How do I make my mark? How do I quickly develop the new skills

I need? Sometimes what can happen is that the new task feels overwhelming and many managers revert to micro-managing.

A dramatic example of this phenomenon being played out in public involved the then newly appointed Chief Executive of Lloyds Bank, António Horta-Osório, in 2011. Appointed with much fanfare and an £8 million package, he was reportedly a self-confessed zealot where his work was concerned with compulsive attention to detail and wanting to ensure that all aspects of the work of his team were up to his own high standards. After only eight months in the job he had to take several weeks of sick leave, when it emerged that the immediate trigger to getting help was that he had spent at least five days with no sleep. One view from the City was that he had underestimated the size of the task involved in turning round a problematical bank and had convinced himself that the only solution was that *he* had to find all the solutions. This sounds all too plausible: a clever and highly competent man trapped by his own obsessive conscientiousness.

Managing that monkey

You do not have to be at such exalted levels of financial reward, seniority, and responsibility to know how it happens. First, there's that familiar head round the door and 'Have you got a minute?' The subordinate describes the problem and tells you that you know better than they do how to resolve it and before you know it you have meekly agreed to doing their job for them. The best-ever description of this phenomenon is in a *Harvard Business Review* article by William Oncken and Donald Wass, entitled 'Management time: who's got the monkey?' (easily and cheaply downloaded from the HBR website, hbr.com).

The 'monkey' is a metaphor for the next move in solving any problem. The article describes a subordinate coming into the manager's office with a monkey on their shoulder, temptingly flattering the boss about his or her assumed wisdom and expertise, and skipping off happily without the monkey because the boss has said, 'leave it with me'. The authors make the point that the monkey should exit with its proper owner – the person who has brought it, otherwise your office quickly becomes crowded with monkeys, many of whom will begin to wilt from lack of attention until your office becomes a resuscitation room for sick and dying monkeys. Subordinates learn helplessness while meantime your boss becomes impatient about what is happening to your own proper work so adds a few downward-leaping monkeys to the pack already inhabiting your office. Sound familiar? Coaching is the solution. If a team member does not know the answer to their problem, then coach them – about what information they might need to solve it, or on what questions they should be asking themselves to solve it, or on their own best hunch about how to solve it. Longer term, all of these are usually better than just taking it on yourself.

On our courses we sometimes hear the comment that 'it's all common sense'. Our response is always the same. Would you prefer something that was not common sense? Actually, for something alleged to be common sense, we notice that it is rather uncommonly practised.

The limits of line-manager coaching

In a book like this, written by three people who are enthusiastic about coaching, there is a danger of implying that coaching is the solution to any managerial problem. But of course this is not the case.

267

Therapy

Like any other approach to line management, coaching has its limitations. It cannot be used when what people need is psychiatric help, therapy or counselling. The boundary is sometimes a little grey here but unless you have counselling or psychotherapeutic training, your coachee will need more than coaching if you see any of these signs, which you can remember with the acronym PIPO:

- **P**ersistent distress in the coachee, unable to stop crying, he or she has overwhelming feelings of sadness and hopelessness, depression or chronic anxiety.
- **I**ntrusive impact on the coachee's life: they tell you they are unable to do their job or live their lives with any pleasure.
- **P**hysical symptoms: they describe sleeplessness, palpitations, drinking/eating problems.
- **O**verwhelming emotion: frequent outbursts, threats to harm self or others.

If you have an in-house counselling service, an Occupational Health Department or an Employee Assistance Programme, they might be able to help, otherwise your coaching should be around encouraging the coachee to get an appointment with their GP as soon as possible. GPs are first and best entry point to mental health services.

Poor performance

Nor is coaching the answer when there are chronic problems of very poor performance. It can certainly be used to explore poor performance (see Chapter 7) but it is not the answer where the problems are extreme. When this is the case, ask yourself how many of these criteria apply to the person in question

	Yes	No
Technical competence is low		
Lost the confidence of colleagues		
Low level of self-awareness		
Severe psychological problems		
Interpersonal problems		
Performance issues could damage the organization		
Low motivation to improve		

The more 'yes' boxes you tick of the above list, the more unlikely it is that coaching is the answer. A formal disciplinary process is probably the only solution. Such situations are often exposed when a new boss takes over and uncovers a long-standing performance problem that has not been dealt with by his or her predecessor:

I took over a training team in our customer service section. I had come from another bank where there was zero tolerance of any behaviour that was not overtly customer-focused. Within my first few hours I had heard about X, a woman in my team whose aggression was legendary. Her colleagues were afraid of her, she was supposed to be training first line manager staff but there were a load of negative evaluations about her courses. She had been challenged by my predecessor and had promptly gone off 'sick' with 'stress' and had accused him of 'bullying' her. She had been back at work for two weeks. I sat in on one of her courses and was appalled. She was not across the material, she alienated the participants, she looked scruffy and unprofessional. I did have a few attempts to apply coaching techniques but I quickly realized it was pointless. She did not have the self-awareness, knowledge, skills or temperament to do the job and should never have been appointed in the first place. Her aggressive responses to my feedback showed me why my predecessor had quailed in front of her, but she didn't frighten me. The only solution was for her to leave before she did any more damage and within two months she was gone – to relief all round.

There will be times when fast action is needed because the organization is in crisis and there is no time for coaching of any kind. This is where quick thinking, giving crisp instructions, and expecting people to follow orders is vital, though coaching will have a role to play later when things are settling down again. All organizations need to make provision for how they would respond in an emergency, and in doing the thinking and planning it will be vital to consult broadly and deeply, but in responding to an actual emergency there is no place for asking people how they feel. There are also everyday procedures where rules must be followed. For instance, where there are issues of safety, whether it is checking for airworthiness in a plane or for adherence to the rule of 'no safety boots, no helmet = no job' on a building site, there is little room for debate and discussion.

Comparisons with executive coaching

When you coach as a line manager, you are essentially working to the agenda set by your organization. The focus is on *performance*. The organization wants people to perform well and to fit in. It wants to preserve the status quo, even when the status quo is about change, because this will be change as determined by the organization. Organizations are essentially selfish even where their purpose, for instance as a charity, is for the social good. They are not that interested (though they may piously allege that they are and some of them do mean it because they can see it makes business sense) in your private anxieties and triumphs. Their concern about your career is limited to how far it is useful for them to keep you on board. This makes coaching as a line manager different from the coaching the three of us do when we are working as external coaches with executive clients. There the focus is *developmental*: it is the client's agenda that counts, even though the organization's agenda also matters and needs to be included in the work. Anything and everything is up for discussion, including maybe the fact that the client is restless in their current role and wants to move on. Clients can trust themselves to be vulnerable and may confide in us about topics that they would be unlikely to mention to a boss, however skilled a coach that boss is. This is because the limits of confidentiality are quite different. For instance, we have been told about worries over alcohol consumption or sexual matters; shaming incidents have been confessed and fragile marriages discussed; difficult childhoods have been described because of their impact on the present. Very senior clients can feel isolated and often welcome discussion about troubling moral issues or their worries about the demands the job makes on them. This is notably different from a coaching conversation with a boss where the essential focus is rightly on performance at work, and you might justifiably worry about telling a boss anything that you fear could damage how he or she sees you, or indeed anything that a boss might feel that they were obliged to disclose to others.

The benefits of coaching as a boss

In this book, our purpose has been to lay out the many benefits of coaching: a more aligned team of engaged and motivated people, better quality decisions that are driven down to the lowest possible level, release of creative talent, and far less stress for you as a boss than when you were trying to do your own job as well as the jobs of those you manage.

Then there is the pleasure of seeing people grow and knowing that you have had a significant hand in the process. This is well described by Sara Wright, Head of Leadership and Organization Development at RS Components (see also p. 247), as she observed the changes in Steve, a long-standing senior manager at the company after he had received training in coaching:

> Steve is a senior leader at RS Components. He has been at RS for over 31 years during which he has experienced much change, including the expansion of the business across the world. His current role has global accountability and he has international direct reports whom he has to manage virtually. Previously, Steve's style was to be directive with his team. He would give clear instructions and had a tendency to be task-focused with low levels of active listening. He had inadvertently created the dependency that resulted in his people coming to him for answers rather than thinking things through for themselves.
>
> Steve gained insight into his own authentic leadership style, recognizing that his motivation was not ego driven and that he welcomes, even thrives, on change. Previously he had had a tendency to hide his personal feelings, but as a result of his coaching training he had the confidence to start revealing his own feelings. The impact has been to gain greater buy-in from his staff

and to generate far more open conversations. Steve has received very positive feedback from both team members and those outside his team, which has reinforced his belief that his role is to achieve through others and not by directing events. Overall, he has more time to coach for success, rather than trying to direct all events. His own comment is, 'My journey has helped enormously in developing high performing individuals and to support my managers to function as a leadership team who truly lead. Whilst I now spend less time directing, I am overwhelmingly impressed by the power of approaches aimed at helping others reach their potential so that they can make a real difference to business performance'.

In fact, the 'leader of leaders' role is usually more enjoyable and less stressful than trying to be the expert on every aspect of your team's work. When you coach people as your default managerial style, you can expect leaps in performance and productivity together with staff who produce many more creative ideas. Because coaching is based on respect rather than on hierarchical authority, relationships improve and work becomes enjoyable rather than a chore. As the RS Components story shows (p. 247), the organization becomes better able to respond to change without trauma, even when people have to be made redundant.

Coaching works because it is based on acknowledging deep-seated, universal human needs for autonomy, competence, and relatedness. When its principles are applied with integrity in the workplace, staff are far more likely to feel engaged and motivated. Motivated staff work harder, produce better ideas, and the organization is generally more likely to perform at the top of its class.

At a time when our economy and whole society seem at risk from forces beyond our immediate control, there has never been a more urgent need to grow talent. Coaching at such times is more than just a 'technique' that you can switch on and off at will. It is a wholly different way of seeing the world. It involves regarding people as capable and adaptable, able to think for themselves, qualities that all organizations need in the people they employ. This new way of thinking includes being prepared to give up old opinions and limiting beliefs about what people can and cannot do. Coaching is an optimistic philosophy because it assumes that we are all infinitely resourceful. Brain science has also shown us that human beings can go on learning well into old age. Coaching is about drawing out that innate capacity.

A book can show you the way but cannot teach you how to coach and there is no one perfect way to do it. Give it a go, be willing to experiment, get some training, develop your own unique style. We promise that the rewards are immeasurably satisfying, for you, for your organization, and for the people you manage.

BIBLIOGRAPHY

Covey, S.R. (1989) *The Seven Habits of Highly Effective People*. New York: Simon & Schuster.

Deming, W.E. (1986) *Out of the Crisis*. Cambridge, MA: MIT Press.

Dweck, C.S. (2006) *Mindset: The New Psychology of Success*. New York: Random House.

Goleman, D. (1995) *Emotional Intelligence: Why it can matter more than IQ*. New York: Bantam.

Hawkins, P. (2012) *Creating a Coaching Culture*. Maidenhead: Open University Press.

Institute of Leadership and Management (2011) *Creating a Coaching Culture*. London: ILM Ltd.

Keddy, J. and Johnson, C. (2011) *Managing Coaching at Work*. London: Kogan Page.

Klein, S. (2010/11) Case study: Health plan-led coaching program leads to improved outcomes and cost savings, *Quality Matters*, December/January, pp. 7–11. Available at: http://www.commonwealthfund.org/Newsletters/Quality-Matters/2010/December-January-2010.aspx.

McGregor, D. (1960) *The Human Side of the Enterprise*. New York: McGraw-Hill.

Morgen, S.D. (1997) *Selling with Integrity: Reinventing Sales through Collaboration, Respect, and Serving*. San Francisco, CA: Berrett-Koehler.

Oncken, W., Jr. and Wass, D.L. (1999) Management time: who's got the monkey?, *Harvard Business Review*, November (with commentary by S.R. Covey).

Peters, T.J. and Waterman, R.H. (1982) *In Search of Excellence*. New York: Harper & Row.

Pfeffer, J. and Sutton, R.I. (2006) *Hard Facts, Dangerous Half-Truths & Total Nonsense: Profiting from Evidence-based Management*. Cambridge, MA: Harvard Business Press.

Rackham, N. (1988) *Spin Selling*. London: McGraw-Hill.

Rogers, J. (2010) *Facilitating Groups*. Maidenhead: Open University Press.

Ryan, R.M. and Deci, E.L. (2000) Self-determination theory and the facilitation of intrinsic motivation, social development and well being, *American Psychologist*, 55(1), 68–76.

Senge, P.M. (1990) *The Fifth Discipline: The Art and Practice of The Learning Organization*. New York: Doubleday.

Sullivan, W. and Rees, J. (2008) *Clean Language: Revealing Metaphors and Opening Minds*. Carmarthen: Crown House Publishing.

Thibodeau, P.H. and Boroditsky, L. (2011) Metaphors we think with: the role of metaphor in reasoning, *PLoS ONE*, 6(2): e16782.

Treacy, M. (2003) *Double Digit Growth, How Great Companies Achieve it – No Matter What*. New York: Penguin.

Your feedback matters to us

If you have comments and questions raised by this book, please visit our websites and follow the contact links:

www.jennyrogerscoaching.com

www.worthconsulting.co.uk

ILM is delighted to validate *Manager as Coach* by Jenny Rogers, with Karen Whittleworth and Andrew Gilbert, and recommend it a text suitable to support the Level 3 and Level 5 ILM coaching and mentoring qualifications.

Coaching requires a developed set of skills, high levels of emotional intelligence and significant hands-on-experience. It helps employees deal effectively with change and find solutions to problems. Because of this, it is fast becoming one of the most popular tools in the manager's tool box.

Our coaching and mentoring qualifications assess formal contracted coaching practice. They are chosen by employers because they enable individuals to learn, grow and deliver their full potential. While focusing on informal coaching activity, *Manager as Coach* shares this vision. It supports our belief that done correctly, coaching is one of the most powerful and cost effective ways of developing individual and organisation performance. Practice is key to developing the coaching skill, whether you are a new aspiring leader or a member of the senior management team. *Manager as Coach* is a practical, step by step guide to acquiring this skill as part of management practice. As such, the book is highly suitable as learner support for those undertaking ILM coaching and mentoring qualifications.

While our coaching qualifications are designed to develop coaching skills through formal coaching activity, this practical book focuses on the manager as a coach and how to use the OSCAR coaching model as part of management practice.

The Institute of Leadership & Management

Overview of ILM

ILM is the largest independent organisation focused on leadership and management. We support organisations in building strong leaders and managers through qualifications, membership and CPD support.

We offer more leadership and management qualifications than any other awarding body though our network of 2,500 accredited centres worldwide. Not only are our qualifications industry-standard, ranging from team leader programmes to diplomas for senior directors, but they help retain and motivate staff too. There are over 130 programmes to choose from, diplomas in leadership through to team leading awards and certificates in coaching.

We also connect a community of 35,000 leaders and managers committed to making a real difference to their organisations. They've become better managers by receiving the professional recognition and management support that comes with ILM membership.

Through real-life application and independent research, we know what makes a good manager and a motivating leader. We're passionate about the difference good leadership and management makes to individual and organisational success.

ILM

- Accredits 2,500 training providers and colleges
- Connects a community of 35,000 managers
- Portfolio of over 130 leadership and management qualifications
- Endorse employer in-house programmes
- Accreditation of training providers
- Commission independent research

THE MANAGEMENT MAP

Manager level	Key competencies	Membership grade	Qualification level (VRQs)	Academic equivalent
CEO and director of large divisions	• Lead senior management team; provide vision and direction for the organization (CEO only) • Provide organizational leadership; build commitment to the vision and values. Develop corporate policy and strategy, lead change, optimize organizational capacity, develop excellence and a customer-focused approach; ensure long-term financial stability and growth. **Underpinned by** critical thinking and research, ability to make hard decisions and solve 'wicked' problems. Knows strategic issues of function specific areas (HR, Marketing, Finance, Operations, R&D)	Fellow	7	Post graduate degree

(Continued)

Manager level	Key competencies	Membership grade	Qualification level (VRQs)	Academic equivalent
Senior manager (departmental/ divisional/functional manager in larger organizations)	• Provide departmental leadership; plan and implement strategies; lead change programmes. • Plan and manage operations, people and resources to maximize effectiveness; monitor performance and control budgets • Encourage innovation, effective internal communications and cross-functional/inter-departmental working; assess and manage risks and contingency planning **Underpinned by:** information analysis and synthesis, financial and performance management skills, and understands key operational issues in function-specific areas (HR, Marketing, Finance, Operations, R&D, etc)	Member or Fellow	6/7	Degree – full and Post graduate degree
Manager – departmental/ divisional/functional manager – in medium-sized organizations; intermediate/middle manager in larger organization	• Provide departmental/divisional leadership; plan, manage, and monitor operations; lead change projects; develop people and resources to maximize operational safety, efficiency and effectiveness; monitor performance and control budgets • Encourage innovation and improvement, set goals and delegate tasks to direct reports, communicate with teams and manage risks	Member	4/5	Up to second year of degree, Foundation Degree or HND

First line manager/ supervisor	• Provide leadership to an operational or functional team; plan and manage workload; communicate plans and objectives and build engagement; manage individual and team performance and development; encourage innovation, support and lead change projects; initiate and lead improvement **Underpinned by:** self-management, team building and performance management skills; information processing skills; an awareness of customers and their requirements, organizational policies and procedures, and inter-personal dynamics	Associate	3	A Level
	Underpinned by: information analysis, financial, people and performance management skills; and an awareness of key issues in other areas (HR, Marketing, Finance, Operations, R&D)			
Team supervisor/team leader	• Provide leadership to a team; plan day-to-day workload, and allocate, and monitor tasks, resolve problems, support change, brief and motivate a team. **Underpinned by:** self-management and team building skills; aware of customers requirements, and inter-personal dynamics	Affiliate	2	GCSE

*NB: Higher level leadership roles imply possession of the knowledge and skills of lower level roles.

INDEX

Locators shown in *italics* refer to boxes and case studies.

INDEX